Hawaii Bucket List Adventure Guide

Explore 100 Offbeat Destinations You Must Visit!

Ian Zuniga

Canyon Press
canyon@purplelink.org

Please consider writing a review!
Just visit: purplelink.org/review

ISBN: 978-1-957590-02-8

Table of Contents

How to Use This Book

Welcome to your very own adventure guide to exploring the many wonders of the state of Hawaii. This book not only offers the most wonderful places to visit and sights to see in the vast state, but it also provides GPS coordinates for Google Maps to make exploring that much easier.

Adventure Guide
Sorted by region, this guide offers over 100 amazing wonders found in Hawaii for you to see and explore. They can be visited in any order and this book will help you keep track of where you've been and where to look forward to going next. Each section describes the area or place, what to look for, physical address, and what you may need to bring along.

GPS Coordinates
As you can imagine, not all of the locations in this book have a physical address. Fortunately, some of our listed wonders are located either within a National Park or Reserve, or near a city, town, or place of business. For those that are not associated with a specific location, it is easiest to map it using GPS coordinates.

Luckily, Google has a system of codes that converts the coordinates into pin-drop locations that Google Maps can interpret and navigate.

Each adventure in this guide includes GPS coordinates along with a physical address whenever it is available.

It is important that you be prepared for poor cell signals. It is recommended that you route your location and ensure that the directions are accessible offline. Depending on your device and the distance of some locations, you may need to travel with a backup battery source.

About Hawaii

Hawaii is located in the middle of the Pacific Ocean about halfway between Japan and the contiguous United States. Until 1894, Hawaii was under the rule of kings and queens; the most commonly known royalty are King Kamehameha and Queen Lili'oukalani. In 1894, the Republic of Hawaii was created with Stanford Dole as the first president, but his rule ended during the nationalism that came with the Spanish–American War in 1898. Due to this nationalist mentality, it took about 60 years for Hawaii to actually become a state; it finally joined the United States in 1959.

The state of Hawaii is made up of 137 volcanic islands that spread out over 1,500 miles. This area is all Polynesian, and there are eight main islands: Ni'ihau, Kaua'i, O'ahu, Moloka'i, Lana'i, Kaho'olawe, Maui, and Hawaii. Hawaii is a very lovely place to visit as it is full of numerous beaches and other outdoor adventurous things to do.

Hawaii also has several major historical sites. On December 7, 1941, the Japanese attacked Pearl Harbor, bringing the United States into World War II. From museums to amusement parks, natural wonders to aquariums, there is so much to see and do in the great state of Hawaii, and it is well worth your time to visit!

Landscape and Climate

The eight main islands of Hawaii collectively make up the entire state. Hawaii is named after the largest of these islands, the Big Island of Hawaii, which means "homeland." Only seven are inhabited, and only six are open to the public. The island of Ni'ihau is managed privately by two brothers named Bruce and Keith Robinson, and access to the island of Kaho'olawe is prohibited. The island is reserved for native Hawaiian cultural, spiritual, and subsistence uses.

Hawaii was formed from volcanic activity that built the islands millions of years ago. Several volcanoes are still active today and can be visited by tourists. Two of them are on the island of Hawaii and are the tallest mountains in the state. Mauna Kea stands 33,500 feet in the sky, which is higher than Mount Everest!

When you think about tropical climates, you will more than likely be envisioning something close to Hawaii. The humidity and temperatures are generally less intense than in states such as Texas or California because of the ocean winds. The high in the summertime is typically around 88°F with lows around 75°F. In the winter months, the high is about 83°F and the lows are around 65°F.

Plant and Animal Life

The flowers in Hawaii are unlike any other in the world. The hibiscus is the state flower. Several botanical gardens and arboretums are open to the public to display the beauty and unique nature of these plants. Since Hawaii is so far away from any other land, it is said that all plant and animal life arrived on the island by wind, waves, or wings.

Hawaii is home to a number of different animals, including several sea birds and other sea creatures. If you plan to go snorkeling, you will get to see the colorful coral reefs up close, along with various kinds of tropical fish, dolphins, and sometimes even whales, just to name a few. The animal life in Hawaii adds so much to the uniqueness and beauty of the state. Each island has a lot to offer. On the island of Kauaʻi, you will even find wild chickens running all over the place.

Culture

Hawaiian culture is treasured and valued on all of the islands. When you come to Hawaii, expect to experience a culture unlike anything else in the world. If you can attend a luau, you will see amazing fire spinning, hear exciting chants, and watch world-famous hula dancing. The rich Hawaiian culture includes much history, folklore, and mythology that is unique to the island.

Hulihe'e Palace

The Hulihe'e Palace is located in the historic area of Kona. This location was once a vacation home for the Hawaiian royal family but has since been converted into a museum by the Daughters of Hawaii. The museum features artifacts and furniture from the original time period of the house. This house was created out of lava rocks and has been owned by various people and families over the years. In 1973, it was added to the National Register of Historic Places.

Best Time to Visit: Closed Sunday through Tuesday, open to the public Wednesday through Saturday from 1 p.m. to 4 p.m.

Pass/Permit/Fees: Admission is $22 for adults and $16 for seniors over 62. You admission is $14 for children ages 5 to 12 and $3 for children ages 4 and under.

Island: Big Island

Physical Address: 75-5718 Ali'i Drive, Kailua-Kona, HI 96740

GPS Coordinates: 19.64018° N, 155.99400° W

Did You Know? Each Sunday, the Hulihe'e Palace has a cultural day with mele and hula. Guests are welcome to celebrate the culture of Hawaii right on the front lawn of the palace.

Kahalu'u Fishpond

This 172-acre attraction is one of four remaining historical Hawaiian fishponds. In years past, there were over 100 of these fishponds across the island of O'ahu, but they have dried up over the years. This particular pond is privately owned, but it's leased out for weddings. There is a wedding chapel as well as a pavilion and garden area. The Kahalu'u Fishpond is commonly referred to as the Kahouna Fishpond. Part of *The Karate Kid Part II* was filmed here. Fishponds were historically very important for the native people of Hawaii because they provided most of their food and were essential to everyday life.

Best Time to Visit: This is not open to the public, but private events can be hosted here by reservation only.

Pass/Permit/Fees: For pricing on events, call (808) 931-4111.

Island: Big Island

Physical Address: Kahalu'u Beach, Kamau Place, Kahalu'u, HI 96744

GPS Coordinates: 21.46605° N, 157.83893° W

Did You Know? The Kahalu'u Fishpond has a semicircular seawall that stretches 1,200 feet long.

Kailua Beach State Park

The Kailua Beach State Park offers guests clear water to swim in, fine sand to relax on, and other facilities to make your day relaxing and enjoyable. Locals and tourists alike use this state park for a number of different outdoor and aquatic activities.

The Kailua Beach State Park is one of the top-rated beaches for beauty on the island of O‘ahu. The turquoise-blue water is stunning, and the powdery white sand is so soft. The area has plenty of parking with great access to the beach.

Best Time to Visit: Open daily from 5 a.m. to 10 p.m.

Pass/Permit/Fees: No fee

Island: Big Island

Physical Address: 412-444 Kawailoa Road, Kailua, HI 96734

GPS Coordinates: 21.39727° N, 157.72717° W

Did You Know? The Kailua area is best known for being a quiet, peaceful area that is far from the busy city center, complete with amazing views and relaxing beaches.

Kalihiwai Beach

The Kalihiwai Beach is well visited by guests and locals, and it's very easy to find. The beach is located at the end of the Kalihiwai freshwater stream, and as a result, it has very calm waters. During the winter, the waves are big enough for expert-level surfers and therefore very dangerous if you are unsure of how to safely surf out in the water. In the summer, however, the water is very calm and perfect for families with young children. Many people enjoy packing a picnic lunch and eating under the shade of the surrounding trees. You can pull your vehicle right onto the beach, so you will not have to worry about a long hike to the water.

Best Time to Visit: Any time of year

Pass/Permit/Fees: No fee

Island: Big Island

Physical Address: 3229 Kalihiwai Road, Kilauea, HI 96754

GPS Coordinates: 22.21608° N, 159.42835° W

Did You Know? The only public toilets at this location are portable bathrooms, but most people prefer to stop at the ballfield for bathrooms and nearby restaurants.

Ka Loko Reservoir

The Ka Loko Reservoir was made by a dam on the northern side of the island of Kaua'i. The water flows from the Ka Loko Reservoir to the Waiakalua Stream and into the Pacific Ocean.

On March 14, 2006, the dam broke after a very heavy rainfall and flooded the town of Kilauea, killing seven people and destroying many homes in the process. Because of this tragic event, dams in Hawaii are now very closely monitored and inspected to ensure the safety of everyone in the area and on the islands.

Best Time to Visit: Fishing in the area is recommended during the hours of 12 a.m. to 12 p.m.

Pass/Permit/Fees: No fee

Island: Big Island

Physical Address: Kapuna Road, Kilauea, HI 96754

GPS Coordinates: 22.17768° N, 159.37794° W

Did You Know? When the Ka Loko Dam broke in 2006, it sent millions of gallons of water into cities, an event that was devastating to the area and the surrounding towns.

Kealakekua Bay

The Kealakekua Bay is located 12 miles south of Kona, and it's a great location for snorkeling, scuba diving, and kayaking. The Kealakekua Bay has beautiful coral and many schools of colorful fish, and from time to time, you might even spot a spinner dolphin!

For people who do not want to get into the water, plenty of picnic areas allow guests to enjoy the views, area history, and the sea breeze, all without getting wet. This bay is the location where Captain Cook first landed on the island of Hawaii in 1778. The historical importance of this beach is very crucial to Hawaiian culture and a very special place for the locals.

Best Time to Visit: Sunrise to sunset

Pass/Permit/Fees: No fee

Island: Big Island

Physical Address: Captain Cook, HI 96704

GPS Coordinates: 19.47985° N, 155.92606° W

Did You Know? There is a white obelisk on the shore that memorializes the death of Captain James Cook.

Kilauea Point National Wildlife Refuge

The Kilauea Point National Wildlife Refuge has a ton of wildlife along with breathtaking views. Behind the wildlife refuge are steep cliffs that drop off into the ocean. The wildlife refuge is conveniently located very close to the city of Kilauea. It's home to a number of different sea birds as well as dolphins, seals, plants, and more. Visitors can see a nearby lighthouse from the Kilauea Point National Wildlife Refuge, and tours are available to get a closer look. The birds that reside in the Kilauea Point National Wildlife Refuge are a great attraction for the number of people that frequently visit this area.

Best Time to Visit: Open Thursday through Saturday from 10 a.m. to 4 p.m.

Pass/Permit/Fees: Adult admission is $10.

Island: Big Island

Physical Address: 3580 Kilauea Road, Kilauea, HI 96754

GPS Coordinates: 22.22915° N, 159.39817° W

Did You Know? Kilauea Point National Wildlife Refuge was recognized by the federal government in 1985.

Kona Coffee Living History Farm

The Kona Coffee Living History Farm is the only one of its kind in the entire country. The historic farm area shows guests how coffee pioneers worked and lived during the 20th century.

This living history farm provides a self-guided tour that gives guests the freedom to wander, explore, and learn exactly how farmers worked to make their world-famous coffee. This attraction brings the history of the time to life and allows guests to see the day-to-day operations of Kona Coffee Farm. The self-guided tours go through the coffee orchard, farmhouse, and coffee mill, with a visitor desk to answer any questions and take payment.

Best Time to Visit: Open Monday through Friday from 10 a.m. to 2 p.m.

Pass/Permit/Fees: $14.99 per person

Island: Big Island

Physical Address: 82-6199 Hawaii Belt Road, Captain Cook, HI 96704

GPS Coordinates: 19.49204° N, 155.91423° W

Did You Know? Kona Coffee is famous for its full-bodied flavor and delicious aroma. Coffee beans from this farm and general area are shipped out all over the world.

Lanikai Beach

Located on O'ahu, many people find Lanikai Beach hard to avoid because it is so stunningly beautiful. Several large rocks out in the distance help to make it a very picturesque place.

The name *Lanikai* means "Heavenly Ocean," and if you visit here, you will understand exactly why. It might be a little difficult to locate this beach because there are not many access signs, but you will know you are in the right place when you find the pillar with *Lanakai* written on it at the entrance.

Best Time to Visit: Any time of year

Pass/Permit/Fees: No fee

Island: Big Island

Physical Address: 982 Mokulua Drive, Kailua, HI 96734

GPS Coordinates: 21.39284° N, 157.71515° W

Did You Know? Pedestrian beach access is located between residential homes down beach alleyways. Six different pathways all lead to Lanikai Beach.

Punalu'u Black Sand Beach

Punalu'u Black Sand Beach is the best-known black-sand beach in all of Hawaii. While the sand is the big feature that draws visitors to the area, sea turtles are another draw. The sand on the beach is made of black lava fragments, and the area is surrounded by rows and rows of coconut palm trees.

Black sand beaches are unique to see and experience, but since the black sand can get hot in the day, many people relax beneath the coconut trees for shade. If you plan to go swimming, be sure to wear water shoes because of the temperature of the sand. Always be aware of the current, and be cautious when entering the ocean.

Best Time to Visit: Open daily 8:30 a.m. to 5 p.m.

Pass/Permit/Fees: No fee

Island: Big Island

Physical Address: 96-884 Government Road, Mountain View, HI 96771

GPS Coordinates: 19.13606° N, 155.50484° W

Did You Know? Many people also enjoy snorkeling, as there are always lifeguards during the daytime hours.

Waiākea Pond

This is the largest natural lake on the island of Hawaii, covering 25 acres in the beautiful mountains. Since there are many mountainous areas, it is difficult for lakes to form in Hawaii, so this is a very rare and special area for the state.

The pond is connected to Wailoa Stream, which makes its way down the Mauna Loa volcano and gathers at Waiākea Pond. The pond empties into the Hilo Bay and the ocean. The pond is regularly used for fishing, and there is a boat ramp nearby. Swimming, water skiing, and other water activities are not allowed. Young children enjoy visiting the Waiākea Pond to feed the waterfowl that gather around the pond.

Best Time to Visit: Any time of year from sunrise to sunset

Pass/Permit/Fees: No fee

Island: Big Island

Physical Address: 799 Piilani Street, Hilo, HI 96720

GPS Coordinates: 19.71610° N, 155.07433° W

Did You Know? The Waiākea Pond was used by Hawaiian locals as a fishing pond long before European missionaries arrived.

Waipi'o Valley

The Waipi'o Valley area offers some very scenic hiking trails with breathtaking views of the ocean. In Hawaiian, the word *waipi'o* means "curved water," which is fitting for the geography of the area. Several Hawaiians used to live in the valley until the time of King 'Umi.

Waipio Valley is not only beautiful but also full of history from the ancient Hawaiian days. There are cliffs up to 3,000 feet high and waterfalls that drop over 1,500 feet. This location has some stunning views, and it's worth taking the hike from the overlook to the beach and back.

Best Time to Visit: Any time of year, open 24 hours

Pass/Permit/Fees: No fee

Island: Big Island

Physical Address: 48-5561A Waipio Valley Road, Honokaa, HI 96727

GPS Coordinates: 20.11445° N, 155.59155° W

Did You Know? For some reason, people like to post on social media that it is illegal for guests to access the valley, but that is false information. The back part of the valley is private property, but it is completely legal to walk down the road to the beach and then return.

Waipi'o Valley Lookout

The Waipi'o Valley Lookout is an overlook that offers a great view of the historic valley at the end of the Hamakua Heritage Corridor drive. Guests are welcome to take a guided tour in a van, hike, or ride horses to discover more about the valley and see everything up close.

You must have a four-wheel-drive vehicle to make the trip, so make sure your car can handle it before you embark on the journey to Waipi'o Valley. Many guests have reported that driving to this location is well worth the time.

Best Time to Visit: Any time of year, open 24 hours

Pass/Permit/Fees: No fee

Island: Big Island

Physical Address: 48-5546 Waipio Valley Road, Waimea, HI 96743

GPS Coordinates: 20.12140° N, 155.58520° W

Did You Know? The Waipi'o Valley Lookout was created to be a sacred place for the Hawaiians. A number of kings are buried in the cliffs on either side of the valley.

Akaka Falls State Park

The Akaka Falls State Park extends for about 11 miles across the island of Hawaii. This park is home to Akaka Falls, a massive waterfall of 442 feet that the state park is named after. Guests can view the park from the waterfall area and the gorge below, which the waterfall empties into.

A trail for hikers extends around the park and offers several different views of this waterfall. You'll also be able to see Kahuna Falls, a breathtaking 300-foot waterfall nearby. A 0.4-mile self-guided loop overlooks both waterfalls and is perfect for hikers of any skill level and for families to enjoy. The entire hike will take about 30 minutes to complete.

Best Time to Visit: Any time of year, open daily from 8 a.m. to 5 p.m.

Pass/Permit/Fees: $5 per person

Island: Big Island

Physical Address: 875 Akaka Falls Road, Honomu, HI 96728.

GPS Coordinates: 19.85535° N, 55.14901° W

Did You Know? The Akaka Falls waterfall is the best-known and most-visited waterfall on the island of Hawaii.

Green Lake

Green Lake is in the center of a crater on the island of Hawaii. It used to be the largest natural freshwater lake in the state, but the water was sadly evaporated by lava flow in 2018.

This area can still be visited by guests, but there is no longer any water for swimming or fishing as there used to be many years ago. A lot of vegetation has overgrown the crater where the lake used to be, and the shade makes it a great spot to go for a swim.

The year 2018 forever changed the appeal of this area because of the eruption of Kilauea.

Best Time to Visit: Any time of year

Pass/Permit/Fees: No fee

Island: Big Island

Physical Address: 14-4860 Kalapana Kapoho Beach Road, Pāhoa, HI 96778

GPS Coordinates: 19.50399° N, 154.83909° W

Did You Know? The entirety of Green Lake was boiled away in less than 90 minutes!

Hamakua Heritage Corridor

The Hamakua Heritage Corridor is a scenic drive that is full of small towns to explore, waterfalls to observe, and gardens to discover. This drive takes you along the Hamakua Coast from Hilo to the Waipi'o Valley Lookout. The day trip allows you to see much of the island with numerous detours all along the drive. The botanical garden at the start of the drive includes 2,000 species of plants from all different parts of the world. The very well-known Akaka Falls and Kahuna Falls are here as well. The drive allows you to really experience the island of Hawaii while moving at your own pace and stopping to see whatever you wish along the journey. This is a memorable drive and well worth it to make your trip even more exciting!

Best Time to Visit: Open Monday through Friday from 9 a.m. to 4 p.m.

Pass/Permit/Fees: No fee

Island: Big Island

Physical Address: 36-221 Manowaiopae Homestead Road, Laupahoehoe, HI 96764

GPS Coordinates: 19.98565° N, 155.23551° W

Did You Know? Drive with caution as you travel this corridor because there are hairpin turns and it can be very dangerous.

Hapuna Beach

This beach on the western coast of the island of Hawaii offers guests fun and relaxation. A great feature about Hapuna Beach is the fact that lifeguards are on duty during the day. Not every beach in Hawaii is protected by professional lifeguards, so this is a great location if you want to take small children into the water and feel safer while doing so.

Hapuna Beach also has several picnic tables, public restrooms, and beautiful white sand, making this one of Hawaii's finest beaches. The conditions are almost always ideal for swimming, snorkeling, bodyboarding, and sunbathing.

Best Time to Visit: Any time of year

Pass/Permit/Fees: No fee

Island: Hawaii

Physical Address: 62-100 Kauna'oa Drive, Waimea, HI 96743

GPS Coordinates: 19.99291° N, 155.82587° W

Did You Know? If you visit Hapuna Beach in the early part of the year, you will be able to see migrating whales in the distance!

Hawaii Volcanoes National Park

The Hawaii Volcanoes National Park is home to some of the most interesting natural occurrences in the entire world. The culture in this area is very rich, and it all involves the two volcanoes located in the park: Kilauea and Mauna Loa.

These volcanoes are about 13,677 feet above sea level, and they are amazing sights. There are several things to do nearby, including short walks, a drive through the scenery, visiting the restaurant or hotel, and shopping at the gift shop. The two volcanoes at the Hawaii Volcanoes National Park are very much active, so it is important always to be aware of your surroundings and follow your tour guide as much as possible.

Best Time to Visit: Visit during the spring when the weather is cool and the park is not as crowded.

Pass/Permit/Fees: $25 per vehicle

Island: Big Island

Physical Address: 1 Crater Rim Drive, Pāhoa, HI 96718

GPS Coordinates: 19.39352° N, 155.30961° W

Did You Know? The entire Hawaii Volcanoes National Park covers about 505 square miles and was designated as a UNESCO World Heritage site in the year 1987.

Lake Waiau

This lake is on Mauna Kea on the Big Island of Hawaii. It stands 13,020 feet above sea level. This is the highest standing lake in the entire state and the only lake on the island. Lake Waiau is small, but its size does fluctuate with the amount of rainfall the area receives.

During the winter, the lake freezes over because it is so high above sea level, and during the summer, it is much smaller than at other times of year. This is an important lake in Hawaiian mythology because it is named after the goddess who used this lake for bathing.

Due to the importance of Hawaiian mythology, this lake is marked as a Hawaiian Sacred Site, and there is no swimming allowed in the lake.

Best Time to Visit: Any time of year

Pass/Permit/Fees: No fee

Island: Big Island

Physical Address: Mauna Kea Summit Road, HI

GPS Coordinates: 19.81259° N, 155.47780° W

Did You Know? Lake Waiau is located just beneath the summit of the Mauna Kea volcano.

Lapakahi State Historical Park

Lapakahi State Historical Park is a 262-acre park along the oceanside that features the restored ruins of an ancient village dedicated completely to the sport of fishing. Several buildings that were previously used by the villagers allow guests to see what life was like during those days.

The Lapakahi State Historical Park was added to the National Register of Historic Places in 1973, and it's a must-see spot for people who love learning about history. There is a self-guided tour that allows guests to take all the time they need to explore the various structures and buildings along the coast.

Best Time to Visit: Any time of year, open daily from 8 a.m. to 4 p.m.

Pass/Permit/Fees: No fee

Island: Big Island

Physical Address: HI-270, Waimea, HI 96743

GPS Coordinates: 20.17489° N, 155.89768° W

Did You Know? At the Lapakahi State Historical Park, there is a small inlet on the shore that scientists and archeologists believe villagers used to get canoes in and out of the water.

Lawrence Lovestock

Lawrence Lovestock is a family compound that has a petting zoo for visitors. Several animals here were saved from terrible situations and given a second chance at life. The animals come to the farm and become part of the family's "lovestock." The motto for Lawrence Lovestock is "Unlike livestock that feeds the body, our animals are called lovestock because they feed the soul." The farm has a variety of animals, from small pigs, bunnies, and birds to goats. There are dogs, hens, and turkeys as well!

Best Time to Visit: Any time of year, open Saturday 1 p.m. to 3 p.m. and 5 p.m. to 7 p.m., and Sunday from 1 p.m. to 3 p.m. and 5 pm to 5:30 pm

Pass/Permit/Fees: $17.50 per guest

Island: Big Island

Physical Address: 66-1304 Mamalahoa Highway, Waimea, HI 96743

GPS Coordinates: 21.45256° N, 157.84854° W

Did You Know? People have left reviews about Lawrence Lovestock saying it is the cleanest, safest, and most fun place for kids to enjoy playing!

Mauna Kea

Mauna Kea is one of six volcanoes in Hawaii and the tallest mountain on the planet, standing at 32,696 feet tall. Mauna Kea is a dormant volcano that last erupted about 4,000 to 6,000 years ago. The peak of this volcano is 125 feet taller than its neighboring volcano, Mauna Loa.

Several ancient Hawaiian towns thrived and survived living around this volcano, their residents using the volcano's basalts to create tools. There are several hotels, restaurants, resorts, and beaches surrounding Mauna Kea that host the many tourists and visitors who come to this area of the island.

Best Time to Visit: Any time of year

Pass/Permit/Fees: No fee

Island: Big Island

Physical Address: 62-100 Mauna Kea Beach Drive, Waimea, HI 96743

GPS Coordinates: 19.99945° N, 155.82567° W

Did You Know? Due to the high elevation, dry land, and constant wind, the summit of Mauna Kea is one of the best places in the world for studying astronomy.

Pacific Tsunami Museum

The purpose of the Pacific Tsunami Museum is to inform and educate the public on the two historical tsunamis that devastated the region in years past, one in 1946 and the other in 1960. Many people are unaware of the danger and the destructive capacity of these storms to the area. The museum informs the general population about what to do in the event of another tragic storm. The other purpose of this museum is to preserve what was left from the time period in this area. There are exhibits and many things to look at to learn more about those tragic tsunamis of the past.

Best Time to Visit: Any time of year

Pass/Permit/Fees: Admission is $8 for adults, $7 for seniors, and $4 for children.

Island: Big Island

Physical Address: 130 Kamehameha Avenue, Hilo, HI 96720

GPS Coordinates: 19.72643° N, 155.08364° W

Did You Know? Tsunamis happen all the time in Hawaii, but the few that cause devastating results for the area are the ones documented and remembered in the Pacific Tsunami Museum.

Panaewa Rainforest Zoo

The Panaewa Rainforest Zoo covers 12 acres of tropical rainforest on the Big Island of Hawaii, and it's full of more than 80 different kinds of animals. This zoo is the only tropical rainforest zoo in the country. It has many plants along with the animals.

From spider monkeys to lemurs, from nene geese to turtles, guests are sure to observe many different animals in this beautiful tropical zoo setting.

The Panaewa Rainforest Zoo has gardens full of orchids and bamboo trees, and a beautiful water garden as well.

Best Time to Visit: Open daily from 10 a.m. to 3 p.m.

Pass/Permit/Fees: Free, donations appreciated

Island: Big Island

Physical Address: 800 Stainback Highway, Hilo, HI 96720

GPS Coordinates: 19.65440° N, 155.07264° W

Did You Know? The Panaewa Rainforest Zoo has animal feedings each day where guests can observe and sometimes even assist, depending on the animal and the danger of working with these creatures.

Polihale State Park

Along the western coast of the island of Kaua'i lies Polihale State Park, which is accessible only via a dirt road. Most people choose to use an ATV to get to the area. The beach stretches for several miles and is referred to as "Queen's Pond."

Guests are not allowed to drive along the beach, but the road to the area does have several potholes and can be difficult to access. The park itself has bathrooms, pavilions, and very little shade. Guests are encouraged to bring their own drinking water, umbrellas for shade, and food.

Best Time to Visit: Open daily from 5:30 a.m. to 7:45 p.m.

Pass/Permit/Fees: No fee

Island: Big Island

Physical Address: Lower Saki Mana Road, Waimea, HI 96796

GPS Coordinates: 22.07947° N, 159.76457° W

Did You Know? This area is very dangerous, so do not visit in the dark.

Pololu Valley Lookout

The Pololu Valley Lookout is located at the very northern end of Highway 270. When you get to this spot, simply step out of your car and soak in the views of the cliffs and black-sand beach below. If you are physically able, a 25-minute hike will take you down the side of the cliff and onto the black-sand beach.

This area experiences very strong ocean currents and is unsafe for swimming. The Pololu Valley Lookout has some of the best views on the entire island of Hawaii.

Best Time to Visit: Any time of year, from sunrise to sunset

Pass/Permit/Fees: No fee

Island: Big Island

Physical Address: 52-5100 Akoni Pule Highway, Kapaau, HI 96755

GPS Coordinates: 20.21064° N, 155.73361° W

Did You Know? The Pololu Valley Lookout is a "hidden gem" of Hawaii, and the hike down to the coast is highly recommended to get the full experience of this beautiful area.

Puako Petroglyph Archeological Preserve

The Puako Petroglyph Archeological Preserve is a large area that protects thousands of lava rock carvings. The oldest carving dates back to 1200 CE. While many archeologists say that the meaning of these drawings is unknown, it is believed that they were used to record births and deaths of people on the island of Hawaii. The Puako Petroglyph Archeological Preserve is found along the Kohala Coast and stretches for 223 acres of land. Many people enjoy going on a 1.2-mile round-trip hike through the area. There isn't much shade on the lava fields, so be sure to bring plenty of water and sun protection.

Best Time to Visit: Open daily from 6:30 a.m. to 6:30 p.m.

Pass/Permit/Fees: No fee

Island: Big Island

Physical Address: 1 N. Kaniku Drive, Waimea, HI 96743

GPS Coordinates: 19.95535° N, 155.85082° W

Did You Know? The Puako Petroglyph Archeological Preserve is a form of art known as "stone art" that's found in the lava fields on the Big Island of Hawaii.

Pu'uhonua o Hōnaunau National Historical Park

Pu'uhonua o Hōnaunau National Historical Park is on the western shore of the Big Island of Hawaii. This park is where Hawaiians who were sentenced to death in ancient times could seek refuge. This was also a place of sanctuary during times of battle or war. This national historical park is the only place on the entire chain of islands where the Hawaiian flag can fly alone, without having the American flag next to it. Covering 420 acres of land, the Pu'uhonua o Hōnaunau park is worth visiting!

Best Time to Visit: Open daily from 8:30 a.m. to 4:30 p.m.

Pass/Permit/Fees: $20 per private non-commercial vehicle for 7 days

Island: Big Island

Physical Address: State Highway 160, Hōnaunau, HI 96726

GPS Coordinates: 19.42157° N, 155.91086° W

Did You Know? The Kapu laws in ancient Hawaiian times were punishable by death. When these laws were broken, Hawaiians could escape to this area for a second chance at life.

The Lyman House Memorial Museum

The Lyman House Memorial Museum in Hilo features the natural history of the area. The house close to the museum was built in 1838 and has been renovated over the years. It is the oldest standing wood-framed building on the entire island.

The Lyman House, located directly across from the Memorial Museum, is full of history and interesting things to discover. In the museum are several exhibits that feature Hawaiian culture, including collections of shells and minerals. The location of the house and the museum make it possible to get a very full and rich understanding of the natural history of this part of the state.

Best Time to Visit: Open Monday through Friday from 10 a.m. to 4:30 p.m.

Pass/Permit/Fees: Admission is $7 for adults, $5 for seniors, and $2 for children

Island: Big Island

Physical Address: 276 Haili Street, Hilo, HI 96720

GPS Coordinates: 19.72244° N, 155.08868° W

Did You Know? The main purpose of the museum is to educate and inform the public of what life used to be like in the early days for Hawaiian natives.

Anini Beach

Anini Beach on the northern shore of Kauai is a great place for people who love to go windsurfing. Another popular activity at this beach is viewing the coral reef that surrounds the island.

The water is anywhere from 4 to 100 feet deep and has been known to have extremely strong currents. Several homes are located long this 2-mile beach, making it a very nice area for both locals and tourists. At the beach itself, there are bathrooms, showers, picnic tables, and a lot of parking. There is not a lifeguard on duty, so enter the water with caution, especially in the winter when the surf is stronger.

Best Time to Visit: Any time of year

Pass/Permit/Fees: No fee

Island: Kaua'i

Physical Address: Anini Road, Kalihiwai, HI 96754

GPS Coordinates: 22.22701° N, 159.46317° W

Did You Know? Anini Beach is one of the safest beaches on the island because the coral reef slows down some of the extreme currents. That means that this beach is perfect for snorkeling and swimming, but always proceed with caution.

Glass Beach

Glass Beach is found in ʻEleʻele, the most industrial part of the island. The beach is made up entirely of sea glass that is the result of years of discarded glass.

The small beads of glass are beautiful and make this a must-see location if you are traveling to Kauaʻi. The sea glass is not painful to walk on because it's been broken up and smoothed over by the ocean water over time.

The "sand" in this condition is a naturally occurring substance that takes about 10 to 30 years to occur, and it's a very interesting sight.

Best Time to Visit: Any time of year from sunrise to sunset

Pass/Permit/Fees: No fee

Island: Kauaʻi

Physical Address: Aka Ula Street, ʻEleʻele, HI 96705

GPS Coordinates: 21.90031° N, 159.58405° W

Did You Know? The pebbles on glass-sand beaches in Kauaʻi are made up of millions of small pieces that are brown, aqua, clear, and blue.

Hanalei Bay

Hanalei Bay is found on the north shore of the island of Hawaii, and it has amazing views of mountains and long stretches of beach to play and relax on. This is the largest bay on the north side of the island, featuring 2 miles of beach on either side of the town of Hanalei.

Since this beach is on the north side of the island, it is a key location for surfers in the winter. The surf and wind are very strong, making very large waves for recreation and observation. During the summer months, however, the area is perfect for swimming, paddle boarding, and sailing.

Best Time to Visit: Any time of year

Pass/Permit/Fees: No fee

Island: Kaua'i

Physical Address: Weke Road, Hanalei, HI 96714

GPS Coordinates: 22.20328° N, 159.50494° W

Did You Know? People have often spotted sharks from Hanalei Bay, so make sure you are always careful when you get into the water, and stay alert at all times.

Hana Road

The Hana Road, known for its scenic views, is one of the top attractions on the island of Hawaii. People travel the Road to Hana to see the whole island in a matter of a few hours. These travelers commonly refer to Hana Road as enjoyable, saying "It is the journey, not the destination" that makes this such a fun attraction. There are curves in the road along the ocean coast, displaying black, red, and white sandy beaches, as well as a number of different trails and gardens that people can observe at various points along their journey. This is a self-guided tour that will help you become familiar with the island and see more than you ever thought possible!

Best Time to Visit: Any time of year

Pass/Permit/Fees: No fee

Island: Kaua'i

Physical Address: Hana Road is accessed from Hanapepe Road, HI 96716

GPS Coordinates: 21.91100° N, 159.58914° W

Did You Know? Hana Road is commonly referred to as the "divorce highway" because it can test your nerves and patience when you drive around 620 curves and over 59 bridges.

Kalalau Lookout

The Kalalau Lookout is a very well-known and well-visited area with breathtaking panoramic views of the ocean and the Kalalau Valley below. If you have seen a photo of a valley in Hawaii, chances are you were looking at an image taken from the Kalalau Lookout!

This area is the main spot where several movies were filmed, including *King Kong*, *Mighty Joe Young*, *Six Days Seven Nights*, and *Jurassic Park*. The Kalalau Lookout stands 4,000 feet above sea level and is well worth the visit.

Best Time to Visit: Any time of year

Pass/Permit/Fees: No fee

Island: Kaua'i

Physical Address: Kokee Road, Kapa'a, HI 96746

GPS Coordinates: 22.15541° N, 159.64528° W

Did You Know? The Kalalau Valley was occupied by a family who farmed crops until 1919. The only way to access this valley is to enter by water on a boat or to take the Kalalau Trail and walk.

Kalapaki Beach

This beach on the island of Kaua'i is a great place to go swimming in the ocean in a protected cove. The bay is in front of the Kauai Marriott Beach Resort, a very nice place to stay while visiting Hawaii.

Kalapaki Beach offers beach space to relax, sunbathe, and play volleyball. Visitors can also watch canoes and large cruise ships come in and out of the harbor, have a picnic lunch, or eat Hawaiian shaved ice in the Kalapaki Beach Hut. There is something here for everyone to do, including professional surfing lessons that are taught in this location all year long. To park at the Kalapaki Beach, guests need to use the upper parking lot at the Marriott Hotel. Public beach access is on the east side of the beach.

Best Time to Visit: Any time of year

Pass/Permit/Fees: No fee

Island: Kaua'i

Physical Address: Kalapaki Beach Access Parking, Lala Road, Lihue, HI 96766

GPS Coordinates: 21.96091° N, 159.35024° W

Did You Know? If you are planning on snorkeling in this area, the best spots to do so are along the edges of the bay because it's relatively bare out in the center.

Kaua'i Plantation Railway

The Kaua'i Plantation Railway offers train rides through the 105 historic acres of the Kilohana Plantation. When aboard the Kaua'i Plantation Railway, guests can relax and enjoy the beauty that surrounds them.

The train ride lasts about 40 minutes and takes you past the various attractions on the plantation estate, including orchards, forests, and farmlands. The point of this ride is to help guests relax and make memories while visiting the great state of Hawaii.

Best Time to Visit: The railway is open Monday, Wednesday, Thursday, and Saturday from 10 a.m. to 3 p.m. Hours on Tuesday and Friday are from 10 a.m. to 6:30 p.m. Closed on Sunday.

Pass/Permit/Fees: $14.99 per person

Island: Kaua'i

Physical Address: 3-2087 Kaumualii Highway, Lihue, HI 96766

GPS Coordinates: 21.97210° N, 159.39186° W

Did You Know? Three different trains run at the Kauai Plantation Railway, all offering enjoyable trips through the 105 acres of historic and beautiful land.

Na Pali Coast State Wilderness Park

The Na Pali Coast State Wilderness Park is on the northwest corner of Kaua'i island. This area is best known for its tall sea cliffs, valleys, streams, and beautiful waterfalls. The Na Pali Coast State Wilderness Park has several walking trails that travel through the park and five different valleys. All along the trail, guests can see a variety of plant and animal life in the area while they soak in breathtaking views. Camping permits are available for the Kalalau Valley, found at the very end of the 11-mile hiking trail. There is hardly any cell phone service or water in the area, so come prepared for a rougher camping experience.

Best Time to Visit: Any time of year

Pass/Permit/Fees: There's no fee for the hiking trail, but camping costs $25 per night for residents and $35 for nonresidents.

Island: Kaua'i

Physical Address: (Kuhio Highway) 6CC9+8R Wainiha, Kapa'a, HI 96746

GPS Coordinates: 22.16717° N, 159.63868° W

Did You Know? For parking, you need to drive to the very end of the Kauai Northwest shore and park at Ke'e beach. The trailhead is about 20 yards away from the parking lot.

Poipu Beach Park

The most popular beach on the southern shore of Kauai is the Poipu Beach Park. Several crescents are connected here to make a perfectly relaxing location for travelers and locals alike.

The beaches are perfect for swimming, wading in the ocean, boogie boarding, surfing, and sunbathing. People are drawn to this area for the crystal-clear water and the occasional spotting of a monk seal out in the water. Due to the shallow waters, this is a great location for small children to enjoy splashing in the ocean.

Best Time to Visit: Any time of year, open from sunrise to sunset

Pass/Permit/Fees: No fee

Island: Kaua'i

Physical Address: 2179 Hoone Road, Koloa, HI 96756

GPS Coordinates: 21.87422° N, 159.45316° W

Did You Know? There are lifeguards on duty, but always be careful when entering the water, especially if you have small children with you.

Princeville Botanical Gardens

This is an excellent location for tasting chocolate and viewing the beautiful botanical gardens on the island of Kaua'i. On the walking tour, guests are welcome to try several different local fruit, honey, and chocolate samples.

Chocolate from the grocery store tastes great, but have you ever had the opportunity to try delicious home-grown and locally made chocolate? The Princeville Botanical Gardens takes guests through beautiful gardens and allows you to try a few different sweet things along the way.

Best Time to Visit: Open Monday, Tuesday, Thursday, and Friday at 9:30 a.m.

Pass/Permit/Fees: Admission is $85 for adults, $35 for children over the age of 2, and free for children ages 2 and under.

Island: Kaua'i

Physical Address: 3840 Ahonui Place, Princeville, HI 96722

GPS Coordinates: 22.19841° N, 159.45492° W

Did You Know? The botanical gardens cover 9 acres of land, and tours typically take three hours to complete.

Sleeping Giant Trail

The Sleeping Giant Trail is a 3.2-mile hiking trail that travels through the rainforest. This trail includes beautiful panoramic views and even has a pavilion and picnic area to stop for a bite to eat.

Native Hawaiian wildflowers as well as other types of plant life stretch along this moderate hike. The trail is accessible all year long, and pets are welcome to join you on this outdoor adventure.

Best Time to Visit: Any time of year, from sunrise to sunset

Pass/Permit/Fees: No fee

Island: Kauaʻi

Physical Address: Trail parking is adjacent to the house at 5750 Kuamoo Road, Kapaa, HI 96746.

GPS Coordinates: 22.06199° N, 159.34350° W

Did You Know? The hike takes you across the "face" of the "sleeping giant," a name given to this area because of a local legend stating that a giant ate a lot at a party, laid down for a nap, and never woke up.

Wailua Falls

Wailua Falls, located north of Lihue, is easily accessible. The Wailua River divides into two streams that drop 80 feet below. The size of the waterfalls depends on the amount of rain received. During high flow, the two falls are often combined into one.

The Wailua Falls are commonly used in films because they are so beautiful and recognizable. A popular television show, *Fantasy Island*, used this area during the opening credits. The Wailua Falls are frequently visited because you don't have to hike to see them.

Best Time to Visit: Any time of year, sunrise to sunset

Pass/Permit/Fees: No fee

Island: Kaua'i

Physical Address: The falls are at the end of Ma'alo Road, Kapa'a, HI 96746.

GPS Coordinates: 22.03822° N, 159.37838° W

Did You Know? Hawaiian legend says that young men and royalty used to test their endurance by jumping from the top of the 80-foot waterfall into the 30-foot pool below. Unfortunately, according to legend, they did not make it.

Waimea Canyon State Park

The Waimea Canyon State Park is a picturesque location for a picnic or hike on a short trail through nature. The area is known for seasonal trout fishing, and there are great locations for pig and goat hunting close by as well.

The Waimea Canyon State Park is ADA accessible, but there is no drinking water out in the park or on the trails, so always come prepared for being in the hot sun. There is a picnic pavilion if you want to stop for lunch, as well as public restrooms, trash cans, a paved walking path, and a scenic viewpoint.

Best Time to Visit: Any time of year, open 24 hours

Pass/Permit/Fees: Admission is $25 for vehicles with up to 7 passengers and $50 for vehicles with up to 25 passengers.

Island: Kaua'i

Physical Address: Waimea Canyon Drive, Waimea, HI 96796

GPS Coordinates: 22.07108° N, 159.66184° W

Did You Know? Waimea Canyon State Park is home to the ohia, a very abundant tree that's dying due to a fungus that is taking over. Hundreds of thousands of these trees have died on the islands.

Waita Reservoir

This reservoir is often called one of Hawaii's "greatest hidden gems" because it is among the largest bodies of freshwater found in the entire state. This lake-like reservoir is seen in several movies such as *Jurassic Park* due to the beautiful backdrop against the mountains.

Many people visit this area for the bass, tilapia, and other types of fish that can be found in the Waita Reservoir. Private fishing charter services are available for visitors to get the most out of their visit.

Best Time to Visit: Any time of year, open 24 hours

Pass/Permit/Fees: No fee

Island: Kaua'i

Physical Address: Koloa Bass Fishing Tour, 3477 Weliweli Road, Koloa, HI 96756

GPS Coordinates: 21.91877° N, 159.44940° W

Did You Know? The Waita Reservoir was first built in the early 1900s to provide water for the sugar cane fields. It used to be known as Koloa Swamp.

Hulopoe Beach

Hulopoe Beach was given the title of "America's Best Beach" in 1997 and has been drawing in visitors for many years because of the sheer beauty of the area. Hulopoe Bay, located on the southern coast of the island of Lanai, has white powdery sand with crystal blue water. For most of the year, the Four Seasons Resort at Lanai is the best place to enjoy snorkeling and swimming. During the summertime, swimming is perfect, but as the year gets closer to winter, the surf picks up and the waves are unsafe for general swimming.

The park has picnic tables, grills for barbecuing, public restrooms, and showers.

Best Time to Visit: Summertime months

Pass/Permit/Fees: No fee

Island: Lanai

Physical Address: 1 Manele Bay Road, Lanai City, HI 96763

GPS Coordinates: 20.74578° N, 156.89739° W

Did You Know? When visiting Hulopoe Beach, make sure you take a 15- to 20-minute hike along the cliffs to the southeast side to view the Lanai Puu Pehe landmark, an 80-foot summit full of history.

Polihua Beach

Polihua Beach is often considered difficult to reach, but you will find it well worth the effort upon arrival. This beach is secluded and perfect for sunbathing and relaxing without being bothered by a large crowd.

To reach this area, you must either hire a tour guide to take you along a 2-mile journey to the beach or rent a four-wheel-drive vehicle that allows you to get there safely. This beach is not safe for swimming because of large waves and strong winds, and there are not any bathroom facilities available for public use.

Best Time to Visit: Any time of year, open from sunrise to sunset

Pass/Permit/Fees: No fee

Island: Lanai

Physical Address: This is an off-road destination. To access the beach, you will need to hike the Polihua Trail, which can be accessed from Polihua Road, Lanai City, HI 96763.

GPS Coordinates: 20.92155° N, 157.03758° W

Did You Know? The Polihua Beach stretches 1.5 miles along the shore and is the longest beach on Lanai.

Haleakalā National Park

The Haleakalā National Park is a place where Hawaiian culture and beauty can shine their brightest. This area is known for its endangered species, volcanic landscapes, subtropical rainforests, and hiking paths through back-country lands. The area is full of endless outdoor adventures. If watching the sunrise interests you, purchase tickets and reserve your spot to witness nature at its finest. This beautiful national park provides guests with ample sightseeing opportunities as well as solitude and time to relax. Always be sure to make a reservation in advance so that you can visit on the desired day at your time of choice.

Best Time to Visit: Open from 9 a.m. to 5 p.m. daily

Pass/Permit/Fees: $15 per person

Island: Mau‘i

Physical Address: This national park does not have a physical address. The nearest address is the Summit District entrance station at 30000 Haleakalā Highway, Kula, HI 96790.

GPS Coordinates: 20.73159° N, 156.12858° W

Did You Know? The volcano in the West Maui Mountains was the first to rise above sea level many years ago, making this a very old park with a lot of rich history.

Hamoa Beach

Hamoa Beach is well known for its beautiful entrance into the ocean with an amazing surfing area, clear water, and very strong currents. The beach itself is surrounded by cliffs everywhere you look, and it only has two points of entry: stairs or a hotel shuttle.

Many people enjoy coming to this beach for boogie-boarding and body surfing. Snorkeling is popular here as well, but guests need to be aware that it is fully exposed to the ocean. This means that it has the potential to become dangerous from time to time with strong currents and possible sharks in the area.

Best Time to Visit: Any time of year, sunrise to sunset

Pass/Permit/Fees: No fee

Island: Mau'i

Physical Address: Haneoo Road, Hana, HI 96713

GPS Coordinates: 20.72132° N, 155.98751° W

Did You Know? Hamoa Beach was taken over by the Hotel Hana Maui in the 1930s, but they keep the area up and make it a beautiful and relaxing place for hotel guests to visit.

Iao Valley State Monument

The Iao Valley State Monument covers 4,000 acres of rainforest and has several opportunities for hiking, sightseeing, and looking at breathtaking views of the Iao Needle. The Iao Valley State Monument also has a nature center and botanical garden.

A 0.6-mile walk along a paved path shows the Iao Needle, which stands 1,200 feet from the floor of the valley below. If you enjoy being outside and soaking in the beauty of nature, then this short nature walk is just for you.

Best Time to Visit: Open daily from 7 a.m. to 6 p.m.

Pass/Permit/Fees: Admission is $5 for nonresidents, though children under the age of 3 are free.

Island: Mau'i

Physical Address: 54 S. High Street, Wailuku, HI 96793

GPS Coordinates: 20.88156° N, 156.54260° W

Did You Know? Most of the Iao Valley State Monument area is covered with rainforests. The trails in the park run along the stream and through the forest.

Kaanapali Beach

Kaanapali Beach is a popular location that offers places to shop or eat, resorts, scenic beach walks, and areas that are perfect for swimming and snorkeling.

The Kaanapali Beach, which stretches for 3 miles, is known for the crystal-clear water and has been referred to as "America's Best Beach." Since the area has a resort, it is a great getaway location for people from all over the world. Along the beach, there are five different hotels and six condominiums with fun outdoor attractions such as cliff diving.

Best Time to Visit: Any time of day from sunrise to sunset

Pass/Permit/Fees: No fee

Island: Mau'i

Physical Address: You'll need to follow unmarked roads to reach the Kaanapali Beachwalk, Kaanapali, HI 96761.

GPS Coordinates: 20.92039° N, 156.70126° W

Did You Know? When visiting the islands of Hawaii, there is always a chance for the surf to change with wind or other weather conditions. To check the safety of Kaanapali Beach, or any beach you are visiting, visit www.hawaiibeachsafety.com.

Kanaha Pond State Wildlife Sanctuary

The Kanaha Pond State Wildlife Sanctuary, which is close to the Kahului Airport, was once a fishpond built by one of two chiefs who previously lived in the area—Chief Kihapi'ilani or Chief Kapi'ioho'okalani.

It eventually became a home for more than 50 different types of birds. The sanctuary is best observed from the end of the paved walkway at the southern end of the area. In 1971, Kanaha Pond State Wildlife Sanctuary was designated a National Natural Landmark.

There is no fee to visit the Kanaha Pond State Wildlife Sanctuary, but it is prohibited for guests to swim or fish in the area.

Best Time to Visit: Any time of year

Pass/Permit/Fees: No fee

Island: Mau'i

Physical Address: Amala Place, Kahului, HI 96732

GPS Coordinates: 20.89238° N, 156.45234° W

Did You Know? The Kanaha Pond State Wildlife Sanctuary covers about 143 acres of land, and the pond is accessible via a paved walkway.

Kapalua Bay

This is one of the most popular beaches for snorkelers because there are often sea turtles and eels in the water. The relaxing sandy beach offers beautiful views and has won several awards for being the most beautiful beach in Hawaii.

People are drawn to this beach for a number of reasons, from the relaxing sandy beaches to soaking in the sun to the numerous water sports available. There is something here for everyone. At Kapalua Bay, a beach activities desk allows guests to rent equipment.

Best Time to Visit: Any time of year

Pass/Permit/Fees: No fee

Island: Mau'i

Physical Address: 99 Coconut Grove Lane, Lahaina, HI 96761

GPS Coordinates: 21.00073° N, 156.66647° W

Did You Know? Kapalua Bay is one of the safest beaches on the island of Mau'i at any time during the year because there is not much change in the currents as the weather changes.

Makena Beach State Park

The Makena Beach State Park is an underdeveloped white-sand beach that is a great location for swimming, surfing, and fishing. Several surfers use this beach in winter because of the strong currents and heavy winds that create large waves.

The park covers about 165 acres of land and includes two beaches, Makena Beach and Pu'u Olai Beach, as well as a dormant volcano. These beaches are not very large, but the Pu'u Olai Beach is one of the only beaches in Hawaii that allows nudity.

Best Time to Visit: Open daily from 6 a.m. to 7:45 p.m.

Pass/Permit/Fees: No fee

Island: Mau'i

Physical Address: 4670 Makena Alanui, Kihei, HI 96753

GPS Coordinates: 20.63258° N, 156.44503° W

Did You Know? There aren't any water fountains at these beaches, so come prepared with bottled water for your day in the sun.

Maui Ocean Center

The Maui Ocean Center is a family-friendly destination with over 5 acres of aquarium land to explore and learn more about underwater creatures. The aquarium has a number of different species, including sharks.

The Maui Ocean Center opened in 1998 as the largest tropical reef aquarium in the Western Hemisphere. The aquarium plans to create artificial coral reefs to introduce to the wild to help the declining natural coral reef growth.

If you enjoy viewing humpback whales, sea turtles, coral reef habitats, and sharks, then a stop at the Maui Ocean Center will be well worth your time!

Best Time to Visit: Open daily from 9 a.m. to 5 p.m.

Pass/Permit/Fees: Admission is $39.95 for adults, $34.95 for seniors, and $26.95 for children.

Island: Maui

Physical Address: 192 Maalaea Road, Wailuku, HI 96793

GPS Coordinates: 20.79383° N, 156.50997° W

Did You Know? The Maui Ocean Center has a number of interactive exhibits that allow visitors to learn more about sea life and the various animals that reside here.

Molokini Crater

This is actually a tiny island in the shape of a crescent that was formed from volcanic material off the coast of Maui. Most guests take a boat from Wailea-Makena and Makena Beach to access the islet. Molokini Crater is one of the best locations for snorkeling in Hawaii, and there are several ways to get to the island through Airbnb experiences and other tour groups.

If you are going out to the Molokini Crater, be aware of your surroundings because there are frequent sightings of the white-tipped reef shark, which closely resembles a dolphin because of their dorsal fins. While mostly docile, they are still present along the bottom of the coral reef area.

Best Time to Visit: Any time of year

Pass/Permit/Fees: Most snorkeling trips and tours will cost anywhere from $100–$200 per person.

Island: Maui

Physical Address: From Wailea-Makena, snorkelers must take a boat out to Molokini Crater.

GPS Coordinates: 20.63127° N, 156.49534° W

Did You Know? Even though there are sharks in the area, it is safe for swimming and snorkeling because the reef helps to protect guests.

Violet Lake

Violet Lake is a very small lake at a high elevation in the West Maui Mountains, or Mauna Kahalawai, measuring only 10 feet by 20 feet. The lake is named Violet Lake because it glows with color that is reflected from the mountains.

In ancient times, the area surrounding the lake was considered a holy meeting place connecting heaven and Earth. This lake served a number of different purposes in mythology and ancient tales from Hawaii. The area is considered to be an "extremely rare gem."

Best Time to Visit: Any time of year, from sunrise to sunset

Pass/Permit/Fees: No fee

Island: Maui

Physical Address: Iao Valley Road, Wailuku, HI 96793

GPS Coordinates: 20.91070° N, 156.59592° W

Did You Know? Violet Lake is home to many endangered species and rare wildlife.

Wai'ānapanapa State Park

Wai'ānapanapa State Park features a volcanic coastline that is both remote and wild. This area is perfect for camping, lodging, and picnicking. Many visitors enjoy hiking on the Hawaiian coastal trail to Hana, where there is a lovely view of a natural stone arch and a colony of seabirds.

There are other stunning things to see here, such as the Hala forest, a religious temple, several blowholes, and a very small black-sand beach. The park at the location is a popular place to stop for a picnic lunch and is well known for the beautiful crystal-blue waters.

Best Time to Visit: Open daily from 7 a.m. to 6 p.m.

Pass/Permit/Fees: $5 per person or $10 per vehicle for parking

Island: Maui

Physical Address: 255 Wai'ānapanapa Road, Hana, HI 96713

GPS Coordinates: 20.786028° N, 156.00242° W

Did You Know? If you want to reserve a campsite at the Wai'ānapanapa State Park, you must make your reservation at least two weeks in advance to ensure your spot.

Wailea Beach

Wailea literally means "the water of Lea," which refers to the goddess of canoe makers. The beach gives off a "resort vibe," which should help explain the beauty and popularity of the area. This is a wide and soft-sanded beach that has amazing views of Lanai in the distance.

During the summer, snorkeling can be very interesting along the rocky outcroppings at the ends of the beach. People love to boogie board and body surf on this beach as well.

Best Time to Visit: Any time of year, open daily from 7 a.m. to 8 p.m.

Pass/Permit/Fees: No fee

Island: Maui

Physical Address: 3894 Wailea Alanui Drive, Kihei, HI 96753

GPS Coordinates: 20.68634° N, 156.44370° W

Did You Know? There are several resorts on this beach, making it very busy during popular tourist months, but it is still worth a visit.

Kalaupapa National Historical Park

Kalaupapa National Historical Park is where King Kamehameha sent those with leprosy in ancient times to keep them away from the healthy population. Due to the isolation and dire situation these people were in, thousands of them died here. The area of Kalaupapa National Historical Park used to be a prison but is now a refuge for those who are cured but forced to live in isolation. The layers of the cliffs along the coastline are breathtaking at sunrise and sunset. The hike down to Kalaupapa National Historical Park is 3.5 miles with 26 hairpin turns and about 2,000 feet in elevation change. This hike is very demanding and recommended for people in good physical condition.

Best Time to Visit: Any time of year, must be 16 years or older to visit

Pass/Permit/Fees: No fee

Island: Moloka'i

Physical Address: 154 McKinley St, Kualapuu, Hawaii 96757

GPS Coordinates: 21.19435° N, 156.96565° W

Did You Know? Fourteen people who used to have leprosy still live in the Kalaupapa National Historical Park area on the island of Moloka'i.

Kualapu'u Reservoir

Kualapu'u Reservoir is found on the north part of the island of Moloka'i. Its name literally means "hill overturned." This area used to be a pineapple cannery village that worked with Del Monte Foods, but it has since been turned into a reservoir for the surrounding area of the island.

The Kualapu'u Reservoir is a 1.4-billion-gallon freshwater reservoir. It is commonly used for fishing, but always follow the signs in the area for your safety while visiting. Most reservoirs do not permit visitors to swim in the water, but boats for fishing are allowed.

Best Time to Visit: Any time of year

Pass/Permit/Fees: No fee

Island: Moloka'i

Physical Address: Kulea Street, Kualapu'u, HI 96729

GPS Coordinates: 21.15859° N, 157.04893° W

Did You Know? The Kualapu'u Reservoir is one of the largest freshwater reservoirs in the entire world, and it has some of the highest sea cliffs in the world as well. A few of these cliffs rise over 3,000 feet above sea level.

Hālali'i Lake

This lake is on the island of Ni'ihau, the smallest island in population out of the entire chain. When the rainy season comes, this becomes the second-largest lake in Hawaii, measuring about 840.7 acres. During times of drought, it is often not even considered a lake because so much of the water dries up.

Hawaiian birds live here, and it's also a popular area for mullet fish farming. Hawaiians bring baby mullets in barrels and help them during times of rain and drought. The fish enter the lake via lava tubes. They are often sold at Kauai and O'ahu markets.

Best Time to Visit: Any time of year

Pass/Permit/Fees: No fee

Island: Ni'ihau

Physical Address: Hālali'i Lake is accessed via unnamed roads in zip code 96769. Po'ooneone Beach is one of the preferred access points.

GPS Coordinates: 21.86227° N, 160.18395° W

Did You Know? The Hālali'i Lake can change sizes so much that it can be considered both the smallest and largest lake in Hawaii depending on the time of year.

Halulu Lake

This lake is in the south-central region of the island of Ni'ihau, and it's the largest natural lake in all the Hawaiian islands. This lake contains 182 acres during rainy seasons but does shrink dramatically during dry periods.

Before the attack on Pearl Harbor, mules and tractors were used to plow trenches into this and other lakes, along with surrounding lands, to keep Japanese planes from landing. As a matter of fact, many of these furrows are still visible to guests today.

Best Time to Visit: Any time of day

Pass/Permit/Fees: No fee

Island: Ni'ihau

Physical Address: Halulu Lake is accessed via unnamed roads in zip code 96769.

GPS Coordinates: 21.86929° N, 160.20657° W

Did You Know? Halulu Lake is one out of 72 lakes in Hawaii!

Lake Kauhakō

This lake was formed in a volcanic crater on the island of Moloka'i. When the volcano Pu'u' 'Uao erupted between 230,000 and 300,000 years ago, this crater was created with a diameter of 1,600 feet by 2,130 feet. At the base of the crater lies Lake Kauhakō, the fourth-deepest lake in the country.

The shallow sections of the lake contain brackish water that is full of oxygen, and that's where most of the plants and animals live. Because of its volcanic nature, the lake is inspected four times each year to test the safety and chemical composition of the water.

From time to time, Lake Kauhakō has a smell that is similar to rotten eggs, and the color of the water changes.

Best Time to Visit: Any time of year

Pass/Permit/Fees: No fee

Island: Moloka'i

Physical Address: State Highway 470, Kalaupapa, Hawaii 96742

GPS Coordinates: 21.26866° N, 156.98006° W

Did You Know? Lake Kauahakō has recent and historic lava tubes flowing into the crater.

Ala Moana Beach Park

If you are looking for a stunning area that offers about half a mile of solid white sandy beaches, look no farther than the Ala Moana Beach Park. Nestled in the beautiful coastline of O‘ahu island, Ala Moana contains several acres full of trees, places to stop for a picnic, grassy play areas, tennis courts, concessions, and much more. The Ala Moana Beach Park is located across the street from the Ala Moana Mall, making it a very popular tourist destination. During the summer, surfers enjoy the waves. The park is perfect for exercise, whether swimming in the ocean or jogging through the park.

Best Time to Visit: Open from 4 a.m. to 10 p.m. daily

Pass/Permit/Fees: No fee

Island: O‘ahu

Physical Address: 1201 Ala Moana Boulevard, Honolulu, HI 96814

GPS Coordinates: 21.29188° N, 157.84499°

Did You Know? The area where Ala Moana Beach Park is found was swampland back in the 1920s before the Ala Wai Canal was developed.

Ala Wai Canal

The Ala Wai Canal in Honolulu is the northern boundary line for the Waikiki tourist area. The reason for creating this canal was to dry the swamps and rice paddies and to provide a drainage doorway for rivers and streams in Honolulu. Several bridges cross the canal, connecting it to the other side of the city.

No swimming is allowed, but people do enjoy fishing in this area. The most popular fish caught are the great barracuda, western Atlantic bonefish, and sixfinger threadfin. The canal runs for 1.5 miles through the Honolulu area.

Best Time to Visit: Any time of year, open 24 hours

Pass/Permit/Fees: No fee

Island: O'ahu

Physical Address: 2015 Kapiolani Boulevard, Honolulu, HI 96826

GPS Coordinates: 21.29040° N, 157.83134° W

Did You Know? The Ala Wai Canal was built in 1928. Its name means "waterway."

Aloha Tower

The Aloha Tower is an iconic structure in Hawaii and one of the most popular landmarks in the whole state. This tower stands 184 feet in the air and offers guests incredible views of the harbor beneath.

The lighthouse in the tower helped mark the land for up to 15 miles away with a clock that is larger than any other in the country.

The Aloha Tower is a beacon to welcome guests to O‘ahu. *Aloha* is written on the walls of the structure.

Best Time to Visit: Open daily from 9 a.m. to 5 p.m.

Pass/Permit/Fees: No fee

Island: O‘ahu

Physical Address: 155 Ala Moana Boulevard, Honolulu, HI 96813

GPS Coordinates: 21.31774° N, 157.89567° W

Did You Know? When the tower was completed in 1926, it was the tallest building on all the islands.

Aloun Farm

The Aloun Farm is a family-owned business that began when six members of the family immigrated to Hawaii. Upon their arrival, the family decided to start a farm with Asian vegetables, green onions, and herbs. Guests can visit the farm to see exactly how these crops are harvested and sold to the public.

Over the years, the business grew, and today it employs over 180 full-time people on a farm covering more than 3,000 acres. The Aloun Farm is very active in the community and works to support the state's agriculture industry. The Aloun Farm is a fun place to visit for the entire family and will help you create lasting memories while visiting Hawaii.

Best Time to Visit: Open weekdays only from 7 a.m. to 4 p.m.

Pass/Permit/Fees: $3 per person

Island: O'ahu

Physical Address: 91-1440 Farrington Highway, Kapolei, HI 96707

GPS Coordinates: 21.37552° N, 158.04444° W

Did You Know? Guests can visit a petting zoo while they are at Aloun Farm.

Atlantis Submarine Waikiki

The Atlantis Submarine Waikiki provides families the chance to go on a submarine ride and view sea life beneath the surface of the water.

When you embark on a submarine experience through Atlantis Submarine Waikiki, you are sure to make memories that will last a lifetime.

The entire experience lasts about 2 hours and shows visitors boats and sunken ships as well as a number of different sea creatures in their natural habitat.

Best Time to Visit: Open daily from 8:30 a.m. to 4 p.m.

Pass/Permit/Fees: Admission is $133 for adults and $66.50 for children.

Island: O‘ahu

Physical Address: 252 Paoa Place, Honolulu, HI 96815

GPS Coordinates: 21.28129° N, 157.83675° W

Did You Know? The Atlantis Submarine Waikiki goes 100 feet below the surface of the ocean. It's the largest recreational submarine in the world.

Bishop Museum and Planetarium

The Bishop Museum and Planetarium is in the historic part of Honolulu on the island of O‘ahu. Founded in 1889, this is the largest museum in the state of Hawaii.

The main feature of the Bishop Museum and Planetarium is a large collection of Polynesian artifacts and natural-history specimens. There are more than 24 million different pieces of history in the museum, as well as over 13.5 million insects!

Best Time to Visit: Open from 9 a.m. to 5 p.m. daily

Pass/Permit/Fees: Admission is $24.95 for adults, $21.95 for seniors over age 65, and $16.95 for children ages 4 to 17.

Island: O‘ahu

Physical Address: 1525 Bernice Street, Honolulu, HI 96817

GPS Coordinates: 21.33339° N, 157.86833° W

Did You Know? To adequately see everything in the Bishop Museum and Planetarium, plan to spend 2–3 hours exploring.

Byodo-In Temple

The Byodo-In Temple is a nondenominational Buddhist temple found on the island of O'ahu close to the Valley of the Temples Memorial Park. This temple was built in 1968 to celebrate the 100th anniversary of the very first immigrants from Japan to Hawaii. It is not an active Buddhist temple but features an 18-feet statue of Lotus Buddha that is covered in gold. On the outside of the building is a brass peace bell, and ponds surround the entire area. The ponds cover 2 acres and are home to large koi.

The entire Byodo-In Temple contains 11,000 square feet and is visited by thousands of devout Buddhists from around the world. The temple is used for weddings and meetings throughout the year as well.

Best Time to Visit: Open daily from 8:30 a.m. to 5 p.m.

Pass/Permit/Fees: Admission is $5 for adults, $4 for seniors over the age of 65, and $2 for children ages 2 to 12.

Island: O'ahu

Physical Address: 47-200 Kahekili Highway, Kaneohe, HI 96744

GPS Coordinates: 21.43103° N, 157.83213° W

Did You Know? The temple is a smaller replica of the Byodo-in Temple in Uji, Japan.

Diamond Head State Monument

The Diamond Head State Monument on the island of O'ahu is called "Leahi" by the locals. The name of this island refers to its resemblance to a tuna's dorsal fin. During the 19th century, the name was coined by British sailors who thought they'd found diamonds on the beach instead of what they actually were—calcite crystals.

Diamond Head is part of a larger system in the Honolulu Volcanic Series that resulted of one of the volcano's eruptions. This exact location, Diamond Head State Monument, is one of the youngest in the volcanic series at an estimated 400,000–500,000 years old.

Best Time to Visit: Open every day except Wednesday from 6 a.m. to 4 p.m.

Pass/Permit/Fees: General admission is $5, and children under 3 are free.

Island: O'ahu

Physical Address: Diamond Head Road, Honolulu, HI 96815

GPS Coordinates: 21.26807° N, 157.79881° W

Did You Know? Diamond Head State Monument stands at 762 feet above sea level at a towering height of 560 feet.

Dole Plantation

The Dole Plantation is a well-known historic pineapple plantation that draws visitors with a number of different activities for the entire family. From a train ride to the world's largest maze, there is something for everyone to enjoy. The train ride is 20 minutes long and takes guests through the plantation, showing various features of the site along the way.

The Dole Plantation offers a garden tour of other crops that are harvested in this area and also provides the opportunity to smell the sweet pineapple scent. Stop for a bite to eat at the Plantation Grille and enjoy the world-famous Dole Whip.

Best Time to Visit: Open from 9:30 a.m. to 4:30 p.m. daily

Pass/Permit/Fees: Admission is $7.25 for adults and $6.50 for children.

Island: O'ahu

Physical Address: 64-1550 Kamehameha Highway, Wahiawa, HI 96786

GPS Coordinates: 21.52665° N, 158.03563° W

Did You Know? The Dole Plantation is a planned village that was designed to house the workers and their families. It covers 20,000 acres of farmland.

Dolphin Excursions Hawaii

Taking a swim with the dolphins is a great way to safely experience nature up close with Dolphin Excursions Hawaii. The tour takes swimmers to the west coast of the island, where spinner dolphins, Hawaiian sea turtles, and various other marine species swim.

The tour takes guests out into the ocean aboard a 34-foot inflatable boat, equipped with a lifeguard on deck in the event of an emergency. The Dolphin Excursions Hawaii team includes marine biologists and other crew members who are experienced in snorkeling and swimming among dolphins.

Best Time to Visit: Open daily from 8 a.m. to 5 p.m.

Pass/Permit/Fees: Admission is $180 for anyone over the age of 18, $135 for children ages 4 to 12, and $2,025 for a private charter. Children under the age of 4 are not allowed.

Island: O'ahu

Physical Address: 85-491 Farrington Highway, Waianae, HI 96792

GPS Coordinates: 21.48272° N, 158.11233° W

Did You Know? Each boat allows only 15 guests, making it a very relaxing environment and allowing visitors to ask as many questions as necessary.

Foster Botanical Garden

The Foster Botanical Garden, which covers 13.5 acres, is one of five botanical gardens found on the island of O'ahu. This area of O'ahu is very popular and draws in locals and tourists with shopping malls, schools, religious sites, and more, making it a great location for the Foster Botanical Garden. The garden includes a number of different plants and trees that are only native to this area, and it all started with 4.6 acres that Queen Kalama leased to William Hillebrand, a German doctor and botanist. The gardens are a gateway to a number of different native plants and animals, mostly birds. Guests can walk through the botanical garden and soak in the beauty and history of the area.

Best Time to Visit: Open from 9 a.m. to 4 p.m.

Pass/Permit/Fees: Admission is $5 for adults and $1 for children ages 6 to 12. Children under the age of 5 are free.

Island: O'ahu, HI

Physical Address: 180 N Vineyard Boulevard, Honolulu, HI 96817

GPS Coordinates: 21.31685° N, 157.85984° W

Did You Know? In the garden are several sculptures and memorial pieces documenting the Japanese influence on the success of the island.

Hanauma Bay Nature Preserve

The Hanauma Bay Nature Preserve includes a beach, sea turtles, parrotfish, and much more. The nature preserve, which is located along the southeast coast of O'ahu, is a very popular tourist destination.

Visitors are welcome to take a snorkeling tour to see the fish and sea turtles up close with a guide who is familiar with and knowledgeable about marine life.

Best Time to Visit: Any time of year

Pass/Permit/Fees: Visiting the nature preserve is free, but snorkeling excursions start at $34.95 per person.

Island: O'ahu

Physical Address: 100 Hanauma Bay Road, Honolulu, Hawaii 96825

GPS Coordinates: 21.27148° N, 157.69629° W

Did You Know? The name *Hanauma* comes from two Hawaiian words: *hana*, which means "bay," and *uma*, meaning "curved." It's a very literal definition of what this bay looks like!

Harold L. Lyon Arboretum

The Harold L. Lyon Arboretum is a 200-acre botanical garden maintained by the University of Hawaii at Manoa. Most of the garden is made up of tropical rainforest plants.

There are several trails for hiking or walking and a number of small water areas. The entire arboretum has more than 15,000 different plants that are both native and Polynesian. There is also an active seed bank at this location.

Best Time to Visit: Open Monday through Friday from 9 a.m. to 3 p.m., close weekends

Pass/Permit/Fees: No fee, but you must make reservations for a "virtual ticket."

Island: O'ahu

Physical Address: 3860 Manoa Road, Honolulu, HI 96822

GPS Coordinates: 21.33357° N, 157.79930° W

Did You Know? There are over 7 miles of hiking trails at the Harold L. Lyon Arboretum, so make sure you wear proper walking shoes when you visit this beautiful botanical garden.

Hawaii Children's Discovery Center

Hawaii Children's Discovery Center was founded in 1989. This museum has more than 38,000 square feet where children can explore, play, learn, and grow. This organization is a nonprofit and has various activities for children of all ages. There are exhibits to help encourage children to learn the various parts of their bodies and how they work together. Other areas address community functions and occupations such as working as a firefighter, mechanic, and art performer. *Hawaiian Rainbows* is all about the culture and history of Hawaii. Children can play, dress up, and learn about many things while visiting the Hawaii Children's Discovery Center.

Best Time to Visit: Open Tuesday through Friday from 9 a.m. to 12 p.m., weekends from 10 a.m. to 12 p.m. and 1 p.m. to 3 p.m., closed Monday

Pass/Permit/Fees: $7–$12 per person

Island: O'ahu

Physical Address: 111 Ohe Street, Honolulu, HI 96813

GPS Coordinates: 21.29456° N, 157.86011° W

Did You Know? The Hawaii Children's Discovery Center is in the building that used to be the Dole Pineapple Cannery location.

Hawaii Plantation Village

The Hawaii Plantation Village is a group of more than 25 sugar plantation buildings and homes from the 1900s. Tours of the interiors of these historic buildings are available to show visitors what life was like.

The Hawaii Plantation Village tells the story of life on the sugar plantations through buildings such as the plantation store, infirmary, bathhouse, and manager's office. The village highlights several cultures from around the world, including Hawaiian, Chinese, Korean and Portuguese elements, to name a few.

Best Time to Visit: Open weekdays only from 10 a.m. to 2 p.m.

Pass/Permit/Fees: Admission is $15 for adults, $6 for children ages 6 to 11, and free for children under 3.

Island: O'ahu

Physical Address: 94-695 Waipahu Street, Waipahu, HI 96797

GPS Coordinates: 21.38563° N, 158.01002° W

Did You Know? The living museum called Hawaii Plantation Village covers 50 acres of land and tells an amazing historical story.

Honolulu Museum of Art

The Honolulu Museum of Art is the only museum dedicated to contemporary art in all the Hawaiian islands. The museum, which opened in 1940, has been collecting modern art ever since. Art enthusiasts will enjoy the various works on exhibit.

The museum also includes a store, restaurant, administrative offices, storage areas, the director's residence, and beautiful gardens outside the museum. The Honolulu Museum of Art covers about 5,000 square feet of galleries full of art.

Best Time to Visit: Open Thursday and Sunday from 10 a.m. to 6 p.m., and Friday and Saturday from 10 a.m. to 9 p.m. Closed Monday, Tuesday, and Wednesday.

Pass/Permit/Fees: $10–20 per ticket

Island: O'ahu

Physical Address: 900 S. Beretania Street, Honolulu, HI 96814

GPS Coordinates: 21.30419° N, 157.84648° W

Did You Know? The Honolulu Museum of Art was designed by Bertram Goodhue of New York.

Honolulu Zoo

If you enjoy visiting zoos and want to spend time observing and learning more about animals, the Honolulu Zoo is definitely something to add to your tour agenda. It contains about 42 acres of land and is home to more than 900 animals. In 1876, King David Kalakaua made lands of the Leahi Crown Holdings available "to the people of Hawaii." Kapi'olani Regional Park was created the following year. In 1947, 42.5 acres of the park were designated as the Honolulu Zoo.

To fully see everything at the zoo, it is recommended that visitors spend anywhere from 4 to 5 hours walking around.

Best Time to Visit: Open daily from 10 a.m. to 3 p.m.

Pass/Permit/Fees: Admission is $8 for adults, $4 for children ages 3 to 12, and free for infants under 2.

Island: O'ahu

Physical Address: 151 Kapahulu Avenue, Honolulu, HI 96815

GPS Coordinates: 21.27208° N, 157.82134° W

Did You Know? The Honolulu Zoo also has an aquarium full of sea animals.

Ho'omaluhia Botanical Garden

The Ho'omaluhia Botanical Garden is a 400-acre area full of tropical plants, a lake, hiking trails, and a free campground. The garden was first opened in 1982 by the United States Army Corps of Engineers with the sole purpose of flood protection.

This garden has a 32-acre man-made freshwater lake, walking trails all around the lake, a visitor center, exhibition hall, workshop, and library. Most people spend between 1 and 2 hours at the gardens and the art show because there is so much to do, see, and experience.

Best Time to Visit: Open daily from 9 a.m. to 4 p.m.

Pass/Permit/Fees: No fee

Island: O'ahu

Physical Address: 45-680 Luluku Road, Kanehoe, HI 96744

GPS Coordinates: 21.38702° N, 157.80388° W

Did You Know? The lake on the property of the Ho'omaluhia Botanical Garden is a catch-and-release lake, meaning if you catch a fish, you must release it back into the water before going home.

Huilua Fishpond

The Huilua Fishpond is one of four surviving ancient fishponds. In 1962, this pond was added to the National Historic Landmark collection after sustaining damage in a 1960 tsunami.

Guests are welcome to visit the Huilua Fishpond and go fishing in this peaceful and relaxing area. This fishpond was a source of food for the Hawaiian people for many years. The fish would enter this reef area, grow, and become too large to leave the pond. The fish would then repopulate, and the people would always have something to eat.

Best Time to Visit: Open daily from sunrise to sunset

Pass/Permit/Fees: No fee

Island: O'ahu

Physical Address: 52204 Kamehameha Highway, Kaneohe, HI 96744

GPS Coordinates: 21.56496° N, 157.87278° W

Did You Know? The aquaculture that occurs in this fishpond area is unlike any other area in the entire world.

Iolani Palace

Iolani Palace was the official residence of Hawaii's monarchy. Now, it tells the history of the islands and offers access to the very halls where King Kalakaua and Queen Liliuokalani walked.

The Iolani Palace, now a National Historic Landmark, was the state's capital building from the overthrow of the monarchy in 1893 until 1969. In 1978, the palace was restored and reopened to the public as a museum with a number of different tours available to give guests the best experience possible.

Best Time to Visit: Open daily (except Sunday and Monday) from 9 a.m. to 4 p.m.

Pass/Permit/Fees: Admission with Chamberlain's Tour is $69.95 for adults and $44.95 for children ages 5 to 12. Tours last approximately 1 hour.

Island: O'ahu

Physical Address: 364 S. King Street, Honolulu, HI 96813

GPS Coordinates: 21.30807° N, 157.85696° W

Did You Know? The Iolani Palace is the only royal palace located on American soil.

Kapi'olani Park

Kapi'olani Park is the second-oldest park in Hawaii and the largest on the island. The park was named after Queen Kapi'olani and covers over 300 acres of land.

The park was historically used as an area for horse racing and was dedicated as the first Hawaiian public space in 1877. The park is home to the Honolulu Zoo and Waikiki Shell. It also has tennis courts; fields for soccer, baseball, lacrosse, and rugby; an archery range; and much more.

Several athletic events are hosted in Kapi'olani Park, including rugby and lacrosse tournaments. It's also the location of several start and finish lines for different road races.

Best Time to Visit: Open daily from 5 a.m. to 12 a.m.

Pass/Permit/Fees: No fee

Island: O'ahu

Physical Address: 3840 Paki Avenue, Honolulu, HI 96815

GPS Coordinates: 21.26658° N, 157.81224° W

Did You Know? Kapi'olani Park is treasured by locals and visitors. It's full of tropical banyan trees everywhere you look.

Keehi Lagoon

The Keehi Lagoon is one of the first beach parks that guests are likely to visit upon arrival in O‘ahu. With its convenient location right next to the Honolulu International Airport, it is frequently visited because of its calm waters for canoeing and boating.

This beach is not ideal for swimming, snorkeling, or surfing, but there is a large grass area for other outdoor sports to be played. This park is a great location for family barbecues and other outdoor parties.

Best Time to Visit: Open daily from 6 a.m. to 10 p.m.

Pass/Permit/Fees: No fee

Island: O‘ahu

Physical Address: 465 Lagoon Drive, Honolulu, HI 96819

GPS Coordinates: 21.33200° N, 157.89688° W

Did You Know? The Keehi Lagoon includes several very small islands, including Mokauea Island, a popular 10-acre fishing location.

King Kamehameha Statue

The King Kamehameha Statue was commissioned in 1878 to memorialize the 100th anniversary of the arrival of Captain Cook at the islands of Hawaii. Standing 18 feet tall and made of solid bronze, the King Kamehameha Statue is worth a visit.

Every year on the Friday that falls closest to June 11 (Kamehameha Day), the statue is given a flower lei to help remember and celebrate the greatest king of Hawaii. King Kamehameha helped to unify the islands of Hawaii when otherwise they would have been torn apart.

Best Time to Visit: Any time of year

Pass/Permit/Fees: No fee

Island: O'ahu

Physical Address: 447 S. King Street, Honolulu, HI 96813

GPS Coordinates: 21.30648° N, 157.85569° W

Did You Know? The King Kamehameha Statue is near the king's birthplace in North Kohala on the island of Hawaii.

Koko Crater Railway Trail

The Koko Crater Railway Trail is a somewhat challenging hike up an abandoned railroad track that is well worth the effort because of the stunning views. The entire hike is 1.6 miles and heavily trafficked.

The trail is often referred to as "Koko Head Stairs" because it's a lot like a workout on a StairMaster! While this endurance-testing trail might seem difficult, all the effort is worth it when you reach the summit and look down at the island of O'ahu. Do not hike this trail if you are unsure of your hiking skill level or are unable to climb several steps.

Best Time to Visit: Open daily from 6:30 a.m. to 11 p.m.

Pass/Permit/Fees:

Island: O'ahu

Physical Address: 7604 Koko Head Park Road #7602, Honolulu, HI 96825

GPS Coordinates: 21.28182° N, 157.69168° W

Did You Know? The trail goes 990 feet up a sharp incline to a summit of 1,208 feet above sea level.

Ko Olina Lagoons

The four Ko Olina Lagoons cover 642 acres and are connected by a mile and a half of pathways along the sea. There is plenty of parking at each of the four lagoons, though it's available on a first-come, first-served basis.

Fishing, surfing, and camping are prohibited on the beaches. These man-made beach coves are the main attraction on the island of O'ahu, and everyone visiting should make an effort to see them.

Best Time to Visit: Any time of year from sunrise to sunset

Pass/Permit/Fees: No fee

Island: O'ahu

Physical Address: 92-100 Waipahe Place, Kapolei, HI 96707

GPS Coordinates: 21.32865° N, 158.12223° W

Did You Know? The first step in creating these Ko Olina Lagoons was to build the rock walls around the perimeter of each lagoon. Once this was done, the dirt was dug out until each was the desired size and then water was pumped to fill them.

Kualoa Ranch

Kualoa Ranch might look familiar to movie-watching tourists because it has frequently been used as a location by Hollywood filmmakers. The area covers 4,000 acres and is used by many for riding ATVs. It also includes a zip line, beaches, and tours of the popular Hollywood film locations.

One of the most popular film tours is the Jurassic Adventure tour, where visitors are shown the exact locations where the films were created while they enjoy the beauty and breathtaking views of the cliffs and beaches.

Best Time to Visit: Any time of year

Pass/Permit/Fees: No fee

Island: O‘ahu

Physical Address: 49-560 Kamehameha Highway, Kaneohe, HI 96744

GPS Coordinates: 21.52169° N, 57.83730° W

Did You Know? If you are visiting Kualoa Ranch, plan to spend anywhere from 1 to 2.5 hours here to make sure you have time to see all the different things this area has to offer.

Kuhio Beach Park

Kuhio Beach Park on O'ahu is a popular surfing spot for bodyboarders. Surfboards are not allowed in this area, but it's not far to reach two popular surfing areas: Queens and Canoes.

This park boasts several historic statues and monuments as well as a beautiful beach to relax on. Several years ago, a lot of construction work was done to keep the beach from disappearing due to the forces of the ocean. About 24,000 cubic yards of sand were added to the beach to keep it as a tourist destination.

Best Time to Visit: Any time of year

Pass/Permit/Fees: No fee

Island: O'ahu

Physical Address: 2453 Kalakaua Avenue, Honolulu, HI 96815

GPS Coordinates: 21.27343° N, 157.82407° W

Did You Know? Kuhio Beach Park is often referred to as "Kuhio Ponds" because the beach is divided by two concrete walls stretching 40 yards into the ocean. Due to this, the water in this area is very calm for families and children.

Laysan Lake

Laysan Lake is a small lake in the center of a tiny island. This is the only lake located in the island chain and only one of five natural lakes in the entire state of Hawaii. Covering 100 acres, it's a freshwater body surrounded by an atoll. The lake is the northwestern part of the Hawaiian islands. The freshwater floats on top of the saltwater, and the tallest point on the entire island is 50 feet above sea level. The island is currently uninhabited, and unfortunately, trash from passing boats frequently washes up on the shoreline.

Best Time to Visit: Any time of year

Pass/Permit/Fees: No fee

Island: O'ahu

Physical Address: The only way to get to Laysan Lake is by boat from one of the other northwestern Hawaiian islands.

GPS Coordinates: 25.77296° N, 171.73543° W

Did You Know? While fishing, swimming, and other activities are not allowed on the lake, Laysan Lake is one of the best snorkeling locations in the entire world. The most difficult part of the experience is getting to the island in the first place.

Lyon Arboretum and Manoa Falls

Lyon Arboretum and Manoa Falls offer more than 5,000 different plants and animal species for viewing by visitors. The arboretum stretches over 194 acres and is full of beautiful plant life everywhere you look.

The Lyon Arboretum and Manoa Falls, which are part of the University of Hawaii, offer several hiking opportunities as well. There are even events for families to help deepen appreciation for plant life and expand their knowledge of the trees and flowers found in this area.

Best Time to Visit: Open weekdays from 9 a.m. to 3 p.m.

Pass/Permit/Fees: $10 per person

Island: O'ahu

Physical Address: 3860 Manoa Road, Honolulu, HI 96822

GPS Coordinates: 21.33421° N, 157.80025° W

Did You Know? Manoa Falls is the smallest waterfall in the state of Hawaii at only 150 feet high.

Mahuka Heiau State Historic Site

Mahuka Heiau State Historic Site commemorates a 2-acre heiau—an ancient Hawaiian temple—on the northern shore of O'ahu. This state historic site overlooks the Waimea Bay and Waimea Valley and offers stunning views. The location of the Mahuka Heiau State Historic Site was perfect for monitoring the entire shoreline with its incoming and outgoing traffic.

Today, guests cannot see the temple itself but only where it used to be. The Mahuka Heiau State Historic Site was added to the National Register of Historic Places in 1966.

Best Time to Visit: Open daily from 7 a.m. to 5:30 p.m.

Pass/Permit/Fees: No fee

Island: O'ahu

Physical Address: 59-818 Kamehameha Highway #96712, Haleiwa, HI 96712

GPS Coordinates: 21.64245° N, 158.05541° W

Did You Know? The heiau played a very large role in the lives of Hawaiians politically, socially, and religiously.

Mission Houses Museum

The Mission Houses Museum in Honolulu was created by the Hawaiian Mission Children's Society in 1920. This museum exhibits many different artifacts, records, documents, and more from the missionary time period of 1820 to 1863. The museum holds more than 12,000 books, manuscripts, letters, diary entries, journals, illustrations, church records, and other artifacts. Visiting the Mission Houses Museum gives guests a closer look at the time period and allows a richer and deeper understanding of everyday life during this time.

Best Time to Visit: Tours are available on Tuesday and Friday at 11 a.m. and 1 p.m., or on Saturday from 11 a.m., 1 p.m., and 3 p.m. Tours are for four people only, so reservations are highly recommended.

Pass/Permit/Fees: Admission is $12 for adults and $5 for students.

Island: O'ahu

Physical Address: 553 S. King Street, Honolulu, HI 96813

GPS Coordinates: 21.30503° N, 157.85622° W

Did You Know? The Mission Houses Museum includes some of the oldest houses in Honolulu, providing a link to the culture of the time period covered.

Nakalele Blowhole

At the Nakalele Blowhole, also referred to as the Halona Blowhole Lookout, guests can witness a natural phenomenon where water soars into the air out of a lava tube. This is a lot like a geyser, but it is unique to Hawaii because it comes directly out of the ocean.

It is advised that you observe the Nakalele Blowhole from a distance so that you and your loved ones are not hurt when the water shoots out. Due to pressure, the water can reach up to 30 feet in height. When this happens, the waves surrounding the blowhole tend to be very strong, so keep your distance and observe from afar.

Best Time to Visit: Any time of year

Pass/Permit/Fees: No fee

Island: O'ahu

Physical Address: 8483 HI-72, Honolulu. HI 96825

GPS Coordinates: 21.28327° N, 157.67668° W

Did You Know? Six people have lost their lives due to being swept out to sea at the location of the Nakalele Blowhole. It is completely safe to visit as long as you follow instructions and do not get too close.

Nalo Keiki Paniolo

Nalo Keiki Paniolo, or NKP, is a locally owned horse farm that offers visitors riding lessons, a visit to their petting zoo, or group rides through Hawaii. The farm features a large outdoor riding area where you can learn how to ride a horse before hitting the trails of Hawaii.

Every Wednesday and Friday, there are several animals available for the petting zoo, including mini goats, donkeys, sheep, and others. The Nalo Keiki Paniolo is a great location for hosting company events, BBQs, or birthday parties. Whatever your occasion is, NKP is here for you to make your day extra special.

Best Time to Visit: Open from 9 a.m. to 6 p.m. every day except Friday and Monday

Pass/Permit/Fees: Prices vary depending on what you do, but a single riding lesson is $60.

Island: O‘ahu

Physical Address: 41-632 Mokulama Street, Waimanalo, HI 96795

GPS Coordinates: 21.34168° N, 157.72123° W

Did You Know? Nalo Keiki Paniolo also offers mini-goat yoga every Friday morning for 1 hour.

North Shore

Surfing in Hawaii is a competitive and exciting sport. In Hawaii, it is most often done on the North Shore of O'ahu. The North Shore hosts several professional surfing events at Waimea Bay and Sunset Beach. Most surfing events take place in the winter because the waves are stronger then. During the summer, there are still things to do for guests and locals because the water is much calmer. It's perfect for snorkeling and observing the colorful reef and fish in the area. In addition to beaches and surfing, you'll find restaurants, shopping, and even the Dole Plantation, where you can tour the facility. North Shore encompasses a large area with multiple beaches, parks, and scenic stops.

Best Time to Visit: Any time of year

Pass/Permit/Fees: No fee

Island: O'ahu

Physical Address: 'Āweoweo Beach Park, 68-197 Au Street, Waialua, HI 96791.

GPS Coordinates: 21.57730° N, 158.15118° W

Did You Know? Depending on the time of year, the North Shore can be very dangerous for inexperienced surfers and swimmers, so always be cautious when entering the water in this area.

Nu‘uanu Reservoir

This reservoir is one of the very few freshwater sources in Hawaii. The Nu‘uanu Reservoir is easy to hike and offers beautiful views of the Ko‘olau Mountains. Created in the late 1800s, it used to be a popular fishing location for guests and locals. You are no longer allowed to fish in the area, and the water is gated off with restricted access. While getting into the water is forbidden, taking a hike around the base of the reservoir is not only relaxing but also highly recommended. Along the hike, you will find a stunning 50-foot waterfall that lands in a shallow pool below.

Best Time to Visit: Any time of year

Pass/Permit/Fees: No fee

Island: O‘ahu

Physical Address: Nu‘uanu Pali State Wayside, Pali Highway, Honolulu, HI 96817

GPS Coordinates: 21.35474° N, 157.80645° W

Did You Know? Several tragic deaths have occurred in this area. One man died from jumping over 50 feet into the reservoir from the water tower.

Paki Community Park

If you need some outdoor fun without going to the beach, a visit to Paki Community Park might be just what you are looking for. This park, which is the perfect picnic location, is conveniently close to Waikiki.

At the Paki Community Park, there is plenty of parking along the street as well as a playground for small children. A fence surrounding the park allows children to stay enclosed in a safe area while playing. With a public restroom, plenty of shade, and even a lovely view of the giraffe house at the nearby Honolulu Zoo, this park is a great location!

Best Time to Visit: Open daily from 10 a.m. to 5 p.m.

Pass/Permit/Fees: No fee

Island: O‘ahu

Physical Address: 3503 Leahi Avenue, Honolulu, HI 96815

GPS Coordinates: 21.27208° N, 157.81380° W

Did You Know? The Paki Community Park also has space for several outdoor sporting activities, including basketball and volleyball courts.

Paradise Cove Beach

This small, sandy beach covered with beautiful palm trees is the perfect spot for soaking up the sun or swimming in the ocean.

Paradise Cove Beach, which is frequently used for wedding ceremonies, is an area where visitors can almost always spot a sea turtle on the sand or in the water. In this bay area, the wind is minimal, and the bright turquoise water is stunning against the white sand.

If you are looking for a perfect location for family photos to document your trip to Hawaii, then visit Paradise Cove Beach.

Best Time to Visit: Any time of year

Pass/Permit/Fees: No fee

Island: O‘ahu

Physical Address: 92-1089 Aliinui Drive, Kapolei, HI 96707

GPS Coordinates: 21.34521° N, 158.12758° W

Did You Know? A luau is held here at sunset every day. It lasts for 5 hours and 30 minutes.

Pearl Harbor Aviation Museum

On December 7, 1941, Japanese planes attacked the American naval base at Pearl Harbor, near Honolulu. The tragic battle ended with the loss of 2,403 lives, including 68 civilians. Pearl Harbor was home to the U.S. Pacific Fleet and 19 U.S. naval ships were damaged during the attack. The attack is the central focus of the Pearl Harbor Aviation Museum, formerly the Pacific Aviation Museum Pearl Harbor. Founded in 1999, the museum allows guests to walk through the history of that tragic day in December. Visitors can expect to spend at least 2 hours touring the battle-damaged airfield and control tower of Ford Island. The museum also boasts two WWII hangars displaying multiple vintage aircraft.

Best Time to Visit: Open daily from 9 a.m. to 5 p.m.

Pass/Permit/Fees: Admission is $25 for adults and $12 for children.

Island: O‘ahu

Physical Address: 319 Lexington Boulevard, Honolulu, HI 96818

GPS Coordinates: 21.36018° N, 157.95959° W

Did You Know? The attack killed over 2,403 servicemembers and injured over 1,178.

Pearl Harbor and USS Arizona Memorial

Pearl Harbor and the USS Arizona Memorial in Honolulu, honor those who lost their lives in the bombing of Pearl Harbor on December 7, 1941.

People come to the museum each year to remember, honor, and learn more about this event. Guests can reach the sunken hull by shuttle boats to view the remains of the battleship.

While it might not be a relaxing day at the beach, the experience will humble you and cause you to pause to appreciate all that the military does.

Best Time to Visit: Open daily from 7 a.m. to 5 p.m.

Pass/Permit/Fees: Admission is $79.99 for adults and $39.99 for children.

Island: O'ahu

Physical Address: 1 Arizona Memorial Place, Honolulu, HI 96818

GPS Coordinates: 21.36887° N, 157.93727° W

Did You Know? On that dreadful day, 1,102 Marines and sailors were killed aboard the USS *Arizona*.

Polynesian Cultural Center

One of O'ahu's top tourist attractions is the Polynesian Cultural Center, where guests can walk through 42 acres of Polynesian history and culture. In the evenings, luaus are highlight the history and culture of the area. The island villages are open for tourists to learn more about the culture through demonstrations, arts, and crafts. The luau includes dinner and a show, which is sure to be something you'll never forget! The Polynesian culture is very important to the Hawaiian people and is a large part of every aspect of their lives.

Best Time to Visit: Open daily (except Sunday and Wednesday) from 12:45 p.m. to 9 p.m.

Pass/Permit/Fees: Admission is $242.95 for adults and $194.36 for children.

Island: O'ahu

Physical Address: 55-370 Kamehameha Highway, Laie, HI 96762

GPS Coordinates: 21.64126° N, 157.91881° W

Did You Know? The Polynesian Cultural Center was opened to the public on October 12, 1963. It has been doing luau shows with up to 600 guests ever since!

Queen Emma Summer Palace

The Queen Emma Summer Palace is a 19th-century home that has been turned into a museum. At the Queen Emma Summer Palace, visitors can see koa-wood furniture that was original to the house, as well as decorations, portraits, quilts, and other artifacts from the royalty of Hawaii's past. Queen Emma, the wife of Kamehameha IV, was very important to the culture and history of Hawaii. Visiting her summer retreat allows the public to better understand who she was as a person.

Best Time to Visit: Open daily (except Sunday and Monday) from 9:30 a.m. to 4 p.m.

Pass/Permit/Fees: Admission is $10 for adults, $8 for seniors or children ages 5 and up, and free for children under the age of 5.

Island: O'ahu

Physical Address: 2913 Pali Highway, Honolulu, HI 96817

GPS Coordinates: 21.33685° N, 157.83712° W

Did You Know? The Queen Emma Summer Palace is preserved and managed by the Daughters of Hawaii.

Queen Kapi'olani Garden

The Queen Kapi‘olani Garden, located in Kapi‘olani Park, features a large collection of hibiscus flowers, the state flower of Hawaii. If you visit the area, you will enjoy the sights and smells, regardless of how much you know about plants.

The garden, which opened in 1972, covers 133 acres of land. While the Waikiki area can be very busy, guests find these gardens to be relaxing, and many view it as an "escape."

Best Time to Visit: Open daily from 5 a.m. to 12 p.m.

Pass/Permit/Fees: No fee

Island: O‘ahu

Physical Address: 3698 Paki Avenue #3672, Honolulu, HI 96815

GPS Coordinates: 21.27067° N, 157.81548° W

Did You Know? In 1877, the garden land was donated by King David Kalakaua, who requested that the park be named after his wife, Queen Kapi‘olani.

Sea Life Park

Sea Life Park is on the eastern shore of O'ahu island. This is a child-friendly park that features penguin and sea lion shows, ocean views, and opportunities to swim with dolphins. When the park opened in 1964, it had six interactive exhibits and has since grown to allow guests to work firsthand with these sea creatures.

Best Time to Visit: Open daily (except Wednesday and Thursday) from 10 a.m. to 4 p.m.

Pass/Permit/Fees: General admission is $35.99 for adults and $22.49 for children. Event tickets range from $79.99 to $199.99.

Island: O'ahu

Physical Address: 41-202 Kalaniana'ole Highway, Waimanalo, HI 96795

GPS Coordinates: 21.33261° N, 157.66436° W

Did You Know? The most popular exhibits here are the Hawaiian Reef Aquarium, which is home to several sharks, stingrays, turtles, and fish; the Hawaiian Ocean Theater, where the shows for penguins, sea lions, and dolphins take place; and the Penguin Habitat, to name a few.

Shangri La Center for Islamic Art and Wai'ānapanapa State Park

Wai'ānapanapa State Park features a volcanic coastline that is both remote and wild. This area is perfect for camping, lodging, and picnicking. Many visitors enjoy hiking on the Hawaiian coastal trail to Hana, where there is a lovely view of a natural stone arch and a colony of seabirds. There are other stunning things to see here, such as the Hala forest, a religious temple, several blowholes, and a very small black-sand beach. The park is a popular place to stop for a picnic lunch, and it's well known for its beautiful crystal-blue waters.

Best Time to Visit: Open daily from 7 a.m. to 6 p.m.

Pass/Permit/Fees: $5 per person, $10 per vehicle

Island: Maui

Physical Address: 255 Wai'ānapanapa Rd, Hana, HI 96713

GPS Coordinates: 20.786028° N, 156.00242° W

Did You Know? If you want to reserve a campsite at the Wai'ānapanapa State Park, you must make your reservation at least two weeks in advance to ensure your spot.

Shark Tank Scuba

On the eastern shore of the island of O'ahu is the Shark Tank Scuba adventure, a great way to get an up-close view of these amazing sea creatures. Some island visitors enjoy scuba diving, and doing so with actual sharks adds a lot to the experience.

Inside the Sea Life Park is a shark tank aquarium where trained scuba divers are allowed to explore with stingrays, sandbar sharks, blacktip sharks, and more. If you enjoy being adventurous and want an experience unlike any other, then take a dive into at Shark Tank Scuba. You will not regret it.

Best Time to Visit: Open from 9:30 a.m. to 4 p.m.

Pass/Permit/Fees: Admission is $199.

Island: O'ahu

Physical Address: 41-202 Kalaniana'ole Highway, Waimanalo, HI 96795

GPS Coordinates: 21.31454° N, 157.66315° W

Did You Know? Each year, sharks kill between 8 to12 people all over the world; humans kill over 30 million sharks in this same timeframe.

Twilight Tours

Twilight Tours at the Honolulu Zoo provide guests with an experience unlike any other. When the hustle and bustle of the day is complete, take a Twilight Tour to see exactly what happens in the evening hours at the zoo.

This allows guests to have a more private tour with a guide who can answer any questions you might have about the animals, all without having the heat of the daytime sun.

Best Time to Visit: These after-hours tours are available October through March from 4:30 p.m. to 6:30 p.m. and from April through September from 5:30 p.m. to 7:30 p.m.

Pass/Permit/Fees: Tours are $25 for adults and $20 for children.

Island: O'ahu

Physical Address: 151 Kapahulu Avenue, Honolulu, HI 96815

GPS Coordinates: 21.27208° N, 157.82134° W

Did You Know? Twilight Tours happen whether it is raining or not, so come prepared with an umbrella and poncho in the event of unexpected rainfall.

USS Bowfin Submarine Museum

The USS Bowfin Submarine Museum is a vessel in Pearl Harbor that's open for the public to tour and explore. This museum ship, which was recently renovated, allows guests to observe a variety of artifacts and enjoy a shaded area, gift shop, food options, and more.

The museum educates the public about the history of the United States Navy Submarine Force, a subject that is not frequently discussed or taught. There are several exhibits in the museum, including multimedia and interactive displays.

Best Time to Visit: Open daily from 8 a.m. to 4 p.m.

Pass/Permit/Fees: Admission is $20 for adults and $12 for children.

Island: O'ahu

Physical Address: 11 Arizona Memorial Drive, Honolulu, HI 96818

GPS Coordinates: 21.36939° N, 157.93778° W

Did You Know? The USS Bowfin is 312 feet long and went on nine war patrols between 1943 and 1945.

Wahiawa Reservoir

The Wahiawa Reservoir is a great location for fishing, and it even has a boat ramp for your convenience. Swimming, pets, smoking, alcoholic beverages, and commercial activities are not allowed in this area.

If you are looking for a great place to stop for a picnic lunch, you will enjoy the wooded shoreline of Wahiawa Reservoir on the island of O'ahu. This location is perfect for fishing year round because it is a freshwater area with a picnic table, restroom, trash cans, and a water fountain.

Best Time to Visit: Open daily from 7 a.m. to 7:45 p.m.

Pass/Permit/Fees: No fee

Island: O'ahu

Physical Address: 380 Walker Avenue, Wahiawa, HI 96786

GPS Coordinates: 21.50390° N, 158.05166° W

Did You Know? Wahiawa, known as the "hub" of the pineapple industry, is a place where many people came to work in the fields that grew pineapples.

Waikiki Aquarium

The Waikiki Aquarium, founded in 1904, and has been administered by the University of Hawaii since 1919. It's the second-oldest aquarium in the country.

This location is conveniently next to the Waikiki shore, where there are more than 3,500 different plants and animals to observe and learn about. Several of the nearby schools bring students here for field trips during the year because it is very educational and fun for small children.

Visiting the Waikiki Aquarium is a fun family activity that gives everyone a break from the direct sunshine.

Best Time to Visit: Open daily from 9 a.m. to 4:30 p.m.

Pass/Permit/Fees: $12

Island: O'ahu

Physical Address: 2777 Kalakaua Avenue, Honolulu, HI 96815

GPS Coordinates: 21.26585° N, 157.81971° W

Did You Know? The Waikiki Aquarium is home to the Atlantis Submarine, which allows guests to see the natural coral reef up close.

Waikiki Beach

Waikiki Beach, one of the most popular surfing beaches in Hawaii, is a vibrant and exciting neighborhood in Honolulu. Several high-rise hotels line the shores.

This area includes the Honolulu Zoo, several fine dining restaurants, the Waikiki Aquarium, designer fashion stores, and more. Every beach on O'ahu is open to the public, and no matter which beach you visit, you will have spectacular views and make many memories.

Best Time to Visit: Any time of year, open daily from sunrise to sunset

Pass/Permit/Fees: No fee

Island: O'ahu

Physical Address: 333 Seaside Avenue, Honolulu, HI 96815

GPS Coordinates: 21.27849° N, 157.83407° W

Did You Know? A fun activity to consider while visiting Waikiki Beach is to walk along the shoreline at night. Always proceed with caution and stay as safe as possible, but this is a very relaxing and memorable experience.

Waikiki Trolley

The Waikiki Trolley is a great way to see the areas of Honolulu, East O‘ahu, and Waikiki. More than 50 vehicles transport passengers all over the island, including a few double-decker buses.

If you want to see different parts of the island, the trolley allows guests to hop on and off to see everything in a very convenient way.

Best Time to Visit: Open daily from 8 a.m. to 5 p.m.

Pass/Permit/Fees: Single-line day tours are $40 for adults and $25 for children. Four-day tours are $65 for adults and $40 for children. Seven-day tours are $75 for adults and $49 for children.

Island: O‘ahu

Physical Address: 3015 Koapaka Street, Honolulu, HI 96819

GPS Coordinates: 21.33601° N, 157.90826° W

Did You Know? All the vehicles used for the Waikiki Trolley lines are ADA compliant and come with wheelchair lifts.

Waimea Arboretum and Botanical Garden

Waimea Arboretum and Botanical Garden is a collection of more than 52 different themed gardens. The arboretum and botanical garden contain more than 5,000 species of plant life, making it a beautiful place to visit. These plants are mostly native to Hawaii and are considered to be globally endangered species. The Waimea Arboretum and Botanical Garden offers tours every Thursday and every first and third Sunday of the month. They start at 12:30 p.m. with specialist guides. When you taking a guided tour through the gardens, you will leave the experience knowing more about the native flowers than you ever thought possible.

Best Time to Visit: Open daily from 9 a.m. to 5 p.m.

Pass/Permit/Fees: Admission is $15 for adults and $7.50 for children.

Island: O'ahu

Physical Address: 59-864 Kamehameha Highway, Haleiwa, HI 96712

GPS Coordinates: 22.62693° N, 153.99646° W

Did You Know? The Waimea Arboretum and Botanical Gardens was founded in 1973 and taken over by the National Audubon Society in 2003.

Wet'n'Wild Hawaii

Wet'n'Wild Hawaii is a waterpark in Honolulu on the island of O'ahu. The park stretches out over 29 acres of land and contains a number of different rides and attractions. From water slides to lazy rivers, this park has it all.

Wet'n'Wild Hawaii is the only water park found in the entire state of Hawaii. It's well visited by guests from all over the world. If you are looking for a change of pace instead of sitting at the beach all day, consider this amusement and water park for a day full of fun and splashing!

Best Time to Visit: Open Friday from 10:30 a.m. to 3 p.m., Saturday from 10:30 a.m. to 4 p.m., and Sunday from 10:30 a.m. to 3:30 p.m.

Pass/Permit/Fees: Admission is $35.99 per ticket.

Island: O'ahu

Physical Address: 400 Farrington Highway, Kapolei, HI 96707

GPS Coordinates: 21.33573° N, 158.08641° W

Did You Know? The Wet'n'Wild Hawaii water park is one of the top ten most-visited places for family attractions in Honolulu.

Proper Planning

With this guide, you are well on your way to properly planning a marvelous adventure. When you plan your travels, you should become familiar with the area, save any maps to your phone for access without internet, and bring plenty of water—especially during the summer. Depending on which adventure you choose, you will also want to bring snacks or even a lunch. For younger children, you should do your research and find destinations that best suit your family's needs. You should also plan when and where to get gas, local lodgings, and food. We've done our best to group these destinations based on nearby towns and cities to help make planning easier.

Dangerous Wildlife

You may encounter dangerous animals and insects while hiking. With a good dose of caution and awareness, you can explore safely. Here are steps you can take to keep yourself and your loved ones safe from dangerous flora and fauna while exploring:

- Keep to the established trails.
- Do not look under rocks, leaves, or sticks.
- Keep hands and feet out of small crawl spaces, bushes, covered areas, and crevices.
- Wear long sleeves and pants to keep arms and legs protected.
- Keep your distance if you encounter any dangerous wildlife or plants.

Limited Cell Service

Do not rely on cell service for navigation or emergencies. Always have a map with you and let someone know where you are and how long you intend to be gone, just in case.

First-Aid Information

Always travel with a first-aid kit in case of emergencies.

Here are items you should be certain to include in your primary first-aid kit:

- Nitrile gloves
- Blister care products
- Bandaids in multiple sizes, including waterproof tape
- Ace wrap and athletic tape
- Alcohol wipes and antibiotic ointment
- Irrigation syringe
- Tweezers, nail clippers, trauma shears, safety pins
- Small zip-lock bags for contaminated trash

It's a good practice to also keep a secondary first-aid kit, especially when hiking, for more serious injuries or medical emergencies. Items in this should include:

- Blood clotting sponges
- Sterile gauze pads
- Trauma pads
- Moist burn pads

- Triangular bandages/sling
- Butterfly strips
- Tincture of benzoin
- Medications (ibuprofen, acetaminophen, antihistamine, aspirin, etc.)
- Thermometer
- CPR mask
- Wilderness medicine handbook
- Antivenin

There is much more to explore, but this is a great start.

For information on all national parks, visit https://www.nps.gov/index.htm.

This site will give you information on up-to-date entrance fees and how to purchase a park pass for unlimited access to national and state parks. This site will also introduce you to all of the trails at each park.

Always check before you travel to destinations to make sure there are no closures. Some hiking trails close when there is heavy rain or snow in the area and other parks close parts of their land to allow wildlife to migrate. Attractions may change their hours or temporarily shut down for various reasons. Check the websites for the most up-to-date information.

Made in the USA
Monee, IL
14 February 2024